Story Telling

Bible class activities for ages 2 to 5

Karyn Henley

Child Sensitive Communication, LLC

Karyn Henley's *Story Telling*

Bible class activities for children ages 2 to 5

Written and illustrated by Karyn Henley
Editing and Layout by Kristi J. West

ISBN-13: 978-1-933803-05-0
ISBN-10: 1-933803-05-3

© 2005 Karyn Henley. All rights reserved. Exclusively administered by Child Sensitive Communication, LLC. PO Box 40269, Nashville, TN 37204-0269

Dandelion logo is a registered trademark of Karyn Henley

No part of this publication may be reproduced, stored in a retrieval system, or transmitted in any form or by any means (electronic, mechanical, photocopying, recording or otherwise) without prior written permission.

For more information about this publication, contact:

Karyn Henley Resources
PO Box 40269
Nashville, TN 37204-0269

1-888-573-3953 (toll-free U.S.)

www.karynhenley.com

A word about **photocopying**:

We try to provide high-quality lesson plans at an affordable price for ministry purposes. God has provided us the protection of U.S. Copyright law, and has ordained that "those who work deserve to be fed." (Matthew 10:10). Please do not deprive us of our livelihood by making unauthorized copies from this manual.

Printed in the U.S.A

Contents

Introduction i
A Storytelling Model ii

Stories From Genesis

Creation of Earth, Sky, and Sea 2
  GENESIS 1
Creation of Plants 3
  GENESIS 1
Creation of Animals and People 4
  GENESIS 1
The Garden of Eden 5
  GENESIS 2
Adam Names the Animals 6
  GENESIS 2
Adam and Eve, Cain and Abel 7
  GENESIS 2, 4
Leaving the Garden 8
  GENESIS 3
Noah and the Ark 9
  GENESIS 6-8
Tower of Babel 10
  GENESIS 11
Abraham and Lot 11
  GENESIS 13
Abraham and the Three Visitors 12
  GENESIS 18
The Promise of Isaac 13
  GENESIS 18, 21
Isaac Gets a Wife 14
  GENESIS 24
Jacob and Esau 15
  GENESIS 25
God Talks to Isaac 16
  GENESIS 26
Jacob Deceives Isaac 17
  GENESIS 27

Jacob's Dream 18
  GENESIS 28
Rachel's Sheep 19
  GENESIS 29
Joseph's Colorful Coat 20
  GENESIS 37
Joseph's Dreams 21
  GENESIS 37
Joseph at Potiphar's House 22
  GENESIS 39
More Dreams 23
  GENESIS 40, 41
Joseph's Silver Cup 24
  GENESIS 44, 45

Egypt to the Promised Land

Baby Moses 25
  EXODUS 1, 2
Burning Bush 26
  EXODUS 3, 4
The Plagues in Egypt 27
  EXODUS 7-11
Crossing the Red Sea 28
  EXODUS 13, 14
Israelites Praise God After Crossing
  the Red Sea 29
  EXODUS 14, 15
Bitter Water Turns Sweet 30
  EXODUS 15
Manna and Quail 31
  EXODUS 16
The Ten Commandments 32
  EXODUS 19, 20
Building the Tabernacle 33
  EXODUS 35-36
Twelve Spies 34
  NUMBERS 13, 14

Contents

Aaron's Staff Blooms	35
NUMBERS 17	
Balaam's Talking Donkey	36
NUMBERS 22	
Jericho's Walls Fall Down	37
JOSHUA 6	
The Sun Stands Still	38
JOSHUA 10	
Deborah	39
JUDGES 4	
Gideon and the Fleece	40
JUDGES 6	
Gideon's Men	41
JUDGES 7	
Gideon and the Torches	42
JUDGES 7	
Samson and Delilah	43
JUDGES 16	
Ruth	44
RUTH 1-4	
Hannah and Samuel	45
1 SAMUEL 1, 2	
Samuel's New Coats	46
1 SAMUEL 2	
Samuel Hears God	47
1 SAMUEL 3	

Kings and Prophets

Jonathan Eats Honey	48
1 SAMUEL 14	
David Is Anointed	49
1 SAMUEL 16	
David Plays His Harp	50
1 SAMUEL 16; PSALM 145	
David, the Shepherd	51
1 SAMUEL 17; PSALM 23	
David and Goliath	52
1 SAMUEL 17	
David and Jonathan	53
1 SAMUEL 18	
Abigail Packs Food	54
1 SAMUEL 25	
David and Mephibosheth	55
2 SAMUEL 4, 9	
Solomon's Dream	56
1 KINGS 3, 7, 10	
Solomon Knows About Animals	57
1 KINGS 4, 10	
The Queen of Sheba	58
1 KINGS 10	
Ravens Feed Elijah	59
1 KINGS 17	
A Widow Shares With Elijah	60
1 KINGS 17	
Elijah on Mount Carmel	61
1 KINGS 19	
Elijah and the Cloud	62
1 KINGS 18	
Elijah in a Cave	63
1 KINGS 19	
Elijah Goes Up to Heaven	64
1 KINGS 19; 2 KINGS 2	
A Widow's Oil Jars	65
2 KINGS 4	
Elisha's Room on the Roof	66
2 KINGS 4	
Elisha and the Stew	67
2 KINGS 4	
Naaman	68
2 KINGS 5	
Elisha's Servant Sees God's Army	69
2 KINGS 6	

Contents

King Hezekiah Gets Well — 70
    2 KINGS 20; ISAIAH 38

King Josiah Finds God's Word — 71
    2 KINGS 22, 23

Jehoshaphat's Army — 72
    2 CHRONICLES 20

Taking Care of the Worship House — 73
    1 CHRONICLES 9

Ezra Reads God's Words — 74
    NEHEMIAH 8

Recab's Family — 75
    JEREMIAH 35

Daniel Refuses the King's Food — 76
    DANIEL 1

Daniel Thanks God — 77
    DANIEL 2

The Fiery Furnace — 78
    DANIEL 3

Writing on the Wall — 79
    DANIEL 5

Daniel and the Lions — 80
    DANIEL 6

Jonah — 81
    JONAH 1-3

Jesus' Life, Death and Resurrection

Zechariah Cannot Speak — 82
    LUKE 1

Gabriel Appears to Mary — 83
    LUKE 1

Mary Praises God — 84
    LUKE 1

Jesus Is Born — 85
    LUKE 2

Angels Appear to the Shepherds — 86
    LUKE 2

The Wise Men — 87
    MATTHEW 2

Jesus as a Boy in the Temple — 88
    LUKE 2

Jesus Grew — 89
    LUKE 2; MATTHEW 13

John the Baptist — 90
    MATTHEW 3

Jesus Is Tempted — 91
    MATTHEW 4

Jesus Chooses Twelve Friends — 92
    MATTHEW 4

The Triumphal Entry — 93
    MARK 11

Jesus Washes His Friend's Feet — 94
    JOHN 13

The Lord's Supper — 95
    MATTHEW 26

Jesus' Death and Resurrection — 96
    LUKE 23, 24

Jesus Meets Friends on the Road to Emmaus — 97
    LUKE 24

Jesus Makes Breakfast for His Friends — 98
    JOHN 21

Jesus Goes Back to Heaven — 99
    ACTS 1

Jesus' Miracles

Water Into Wine — 100
    JOHN 2

The Great Catch of Fish — 101
    LUKE 5

Peter's Mother-in-Law — 102
    MATTHEW 8

Contents

Through of Roof   103
    LUKE 5

The Lame Man at the Pool   104
    JOHN 5

The Man's Withered Hand   105
    MATTHEW 12

The Centurion's Sick Servant   106
    MATTHEW 8

Jesus Stills the Storm   107
    MARK 4

Woman Touches Jesus' Hem   108
    LUKE 8

Jairus' Daughter   109
    LUKE 8

Jesus Feeds 5,000   110
    LUKE 9

Jesus Walk on Water   111
    MATTHEW 14

Tax Money in a Fish   112
    MATTHEW 17

The Ten Lepers   113
    LUKE 17

Jesus Heals the Bent Woman   114
    LUKE 13

Blind Bartimaeus   115
    MARK 10

Jesus' Teachings

The Woman at the Well   116
    JOHN 4

Jesus Reads in the Synagogue   117
    LUKE 4

Let Your Light Shine   118
    MATTHEW 5

Birds and Flowers   119
    MATTHEW 6

The Lord's Prayer   120
    MATTHEW 6

The Wise Man's House   121
    MATTHEW 7

Bigger Barns   122
    LUKE 12

Sower of Seeds   123
    MATTHEW 13

Hidden Treasures   124
    MATTHEW 13

The Good Samaritan   125
    LUKE 10

Mary and Martha   126
    LUKE 10

The Lost Sheep   127
    LUKE 15

The Lost Coin   128
    LUKE 15

The Runaway Son   129
    LUKE 15

The Pharisee and a Tax Collector Pray   130
    LUKE 18

Jesus and the Children   131
    LUKE 18

Zacchaeus   132
    LUKE 19

Perfume on Jesus' Feet   133
    JOHN 12

Two Sons and a Vineyard   135
    MATTHEW 21

The Widow's Mite   136
    MARK 12

The Church

Peter and John Heal a Lame Man   137
    ACTS 3

Contents

Philip and the Man From Ethiopia	138
ACTS 8	
Paul to Damascus	139
ACTS 9	
Paul in a Basket	140
ACTS 9; 2 CORINTHIANS 11	
Paul and Barnabas	141
ACTS 9, 13	
Dorcas	142
ACTS 9	
Peter and Cornelius	143
ACTS 10	
Peter Escapes From Prison	144
ACTS 12	
Paul in Lystra	145
ACTS 14	
Timothy	146
ACTS 16; PHILIPPIANS 2; 1 THESSALONIANS 3; 2 TIMOTHY 1	
Lydia	147
ACTS 16	
Paul and Silas in Prison	148
ACTS 16	
Paul's Nephew Hears a Plot	149
ACTS 23	
Paul's Shipwreck	150
ACTS 27	
Paul on Malta	151
ACTS 28	
Fruit of the Spirit	152
GALATIANS 5	
Paul Writes Letters	153
PHILIPPIANS 4	
John Sees Heaven	154
REVELATION 21	

Appendix A

Story Figures	154–155

Appendix B

Shadow Theater	156

Appendix C (Patterns) 157

Leaving the Garden	158
Joseph's Dreams	159
Burning Bush	160
The Plagues in Egypt	161
Deborah	162
Samson and Delilah	163
David and Goliath	164
Ravens Feed Elijah	165
Elisha's Servant Sees God's Army	166
Daniel and the Lions	167
Jesus Is Born	168
Jesus Makes Breakfast for His Friends	169
Jesus Goes Back to Heaven	170
The Great Catch of Fish	171
Tax Money in a Fish	172
Blind Bartimaeus	173
Birds and Flowers	174
The Lord's Prayer	175
Zacchaeus	176
Peter and John Heal a Lame Man	177
Philip and the Man From Ethiopia	178
Peter Escapes From Prison	179
Fruit of the Spirit	180
Paul Writes Letters	181

Topical Index 182-185

Introduction

Story Telling

Young children are wigglers. To hold their attention for more than a few minutes, we have to give them something very interesting to watch or listen to. Or, better yet, give them something interesting to do. Storytelling can be interesting to watch. It can be interesting to hear. It can also be interactive, giving children something fun to do.

There is no reason for story time to be boring for the children or for the teacher! If the teacher is bored and frustrated with the commonly used storytelling methods, then it's highly probable that the children are bored too. And bored children can cause problems.

So, do something different to tell the Bible story each week. Tell stories in ways that are exciting and interesting, because stories can be fun to hear, fun to watch, and fun to do!

A story telling model is included on the following page. This model is included to help give the teacher a sense of how to tell the story creatively.

The Bible stories in this book are not written out word-for-word. Rather, we've included key information and phrases from the story to help you as you tell it. It is recommended that you be familiar enough with the story to retell it in your own words.

Other ideas which will help as you retell a Bible story include:[1]

- Use gestures and facial expressions to reinforce your words.
- Your tone of voice can be incorporated into storytelling. For example, whisper loudly or lower your voice as the story gets more suspenseful.
- Watch for the children's response to you as you tell the story. If children look restless, get more animated and move on to the next part of the story.
- Consider the ages of the children you will be teaching and use words and phrases they can understand.

---

[1] Adapted from *Child-Sensitive Teaching*® by Karyn Henley.

Introduction

A Storytelling Model

Angels All Around
(may be used with activity on page 86)

It was a quiet and still night. On the dark hillsides, the sheep were sleeping and the shepherds were watching.

Suddenly an angel stood in front of the shepherds. (Fly one angel in.) The shepherds were scared. (Ask the children to look scared.)

But the angel said, "Don't be scared. I came to tell you some good news. It will make people happy. Baby Jesus was born today. He's the one God promised to send. He's God's Son. You can go see him. You'll find him in a manger."

Then many angels came. (Ask the children to fly their angels in.) They all praised God. They said, "Glory to God in the highest. Peace on earth."

(ASK THE CHILDREN TO JOIN YOU AS YOU SING THESE WORDS TO THE TUNE OF "MARY HAD A LITTLE LAMB.")

Glory, glory to our God, to our God, to our God.
Glory, glory to our God. Peace on earth to men.

When the angels left, the shepherds said, "Let's go see this new baby." So they went into town and found the manger where baby Jesus was. They told about the angels they had seen. When they went home, they were praising God.

(SING TWO MORE VERSES TO THE SAME TUNE, LEADING THE CHILDREN AROUND THE ROOM.)

Here we go to Bethlehem, Bethlehem, Bethlehem.
Here we go to Bethlehem, to see the newborn King.

Praise our God in Heaven above, Heaven above, Heaven above.
Praise our God in Heaven above, for sending us his Son.

Story Telling

Stories From Genesis

Creation of Earth, Sky, and Sea
Genesis 1: 1-10

Materials
- flashlight
- pan of sand
- small bowl or empty margarine tub
- pitcher of water
- blue food coloring (optional)

Prepare Ahead of Time
- Place the bowl or margarine tub into the sand.

While You Tell the Story

Tell about creation by darkening the room, if possible, and letting a child stand by the light switch. Use the flashlight to make a small amount of light if the children seem to feel scared in the darkened room. When you say "Let there be light," the child at the light switch should turn on the light.

Continue to tell about the creation of the sky. Emphasize two things: how God created simply by speaking the creation into existence, and how God saw that it was good.

Use the pan of sand to tell about the creation of land. Pour water into the margarine tub to represent the seas. Add blue food coloring if you wish.

Talk About
1. When you look at the sky, what do you see? Who made it?
2. Have you ever seen mountains? What are they like? Have you ever gone to the beach? What was it like? Who made these?
3. What is the land like where we live? If you dug into the ground, what would you find? Who made the land?

Stories From Genesis

Creation of Plants
Genesis 1:11-13

Materials
• two pieces of green poster board • string • hole punch

Prepare Ahead of Time
• Make the growing tree by turning the two pieces of poster board horizontally, and placing one above the other as shown.
• Draw a Christmas tree shape that covers both pieces of poster board. Then draw horizontal lines across the tree at intervals of about 5 or 6 inches. Cut out the tree shape. Then cut across the horizontal lines.
• Using a hole punch, punch a hole in the top and bottom of each piece as shown (the hole should be centered from left to right). Thread string through all of the holes, linking the pieces of the tree together, leaving about 2 inches between each piece. Tie the string at the bottom of each piece so it will not slip out. Leave about 10 feet of string clear at the top.
• Loop the string around a high stable fixture in your room (the ceiling struts that support acoustical tile, a cup hook on the back of a cabinet or door, or a curtain rod). If you cannot locate a fixture to hang this string on, use a dowel, and let another adult hold it for you during this part of the lesson. Hold the dowel horizontally with one hand at each end, and loop the string over the dowel.

While You Tell the Story
Tell about the creation of all kinds of plants. Pull the loose end of the string that is hanging over the support you have chosen. The tree rises and sways as you pull the string.

Another Idea: Collect leafy twigs about 5" long from a variety of trees, one for each child. Place dirt or sand in the bottom of a shallow box. Give each child a leafy twig and let them "plant" these trees in the dirt as you tell about how God made plants. Tell about the creation of all kinds of plants, grass and fruit trees that make seeds. Explain how the seeds will grow the kind of plants from which they come.

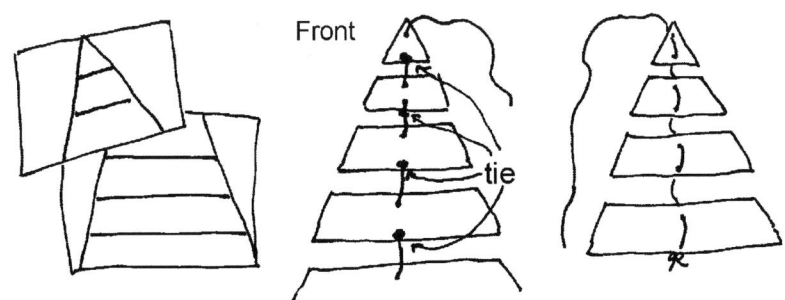

Talk About
1. What kind of plants are around your house or apartment? Who made them?
2. Have you ever grown a garden? How can people make gardens?
3. What grows in a forest? What grows in a field or a meadow? What grows on a farm? Who made plants?

Stories From Genesis

Creation of Animals and People
Genesis 1:20-30

Materials
- a variety of stuffed animals
- chalk, chalkboard (whiteboard or posterboard may be substituted)

While You Tell the Story

Give each child a stuffed animal. As you tell about the creation of animals, let each child make the sound of the animal he is holding. Then he may place the animal at the front of the room.

Review the story of creation so far. After you tell about each item God created, stop and say, "But something was missing." For example, "First God said, 'Let there be light, and there was light.' But that was all. Something was missing." Let the children tell what was missing.

After talking about the animals, tell the children that God made something else. "It had a head like this." Draw a simple circle with eyes, ears, a nose, and a mouth to make a man's head. Continue with his shoulders, arms, hands, torso, legs, and feet. Then remind the children of all the animals God made. "None of those was the special helper that the man needed, so God made a woman."

Encourage all of the children to stand and stretch as you review how God created people with feet and legs, arms and hands and fingers, a head, two ears and eyes, a nose and a mouth.

Talk About
1. What is your favorite animal? Why? Who made the animals?
2. Do you have a pet? What is it like?
3. What color are your eyes? What color is your hair? Who made people?

4

Stories From Genesis

The Garden of Eden
Genesis 2:7-10

Materials
- pen or marker
- a piece of fruit and one or two leafy branches

While You Tell the Story

Make a fist puppet. Place your thumb on the palm of the same hand. Curl your fingers around your thumb. Move the thumb up and down to make the mouth of the puppet talk. With a pen or marker, draw eyes above the mouth. This is Adam. Place a piece of fruit nearby with a leafy branch or two around it to represent the tree.

Tell the story with your fist puppet. Tell the children how God made a man from dust and then created a beautiful garden for the man to live in. God told Adam to eat from any tree except one.

After the story you may want to make fist puppets on the children too, so they can act out the story.

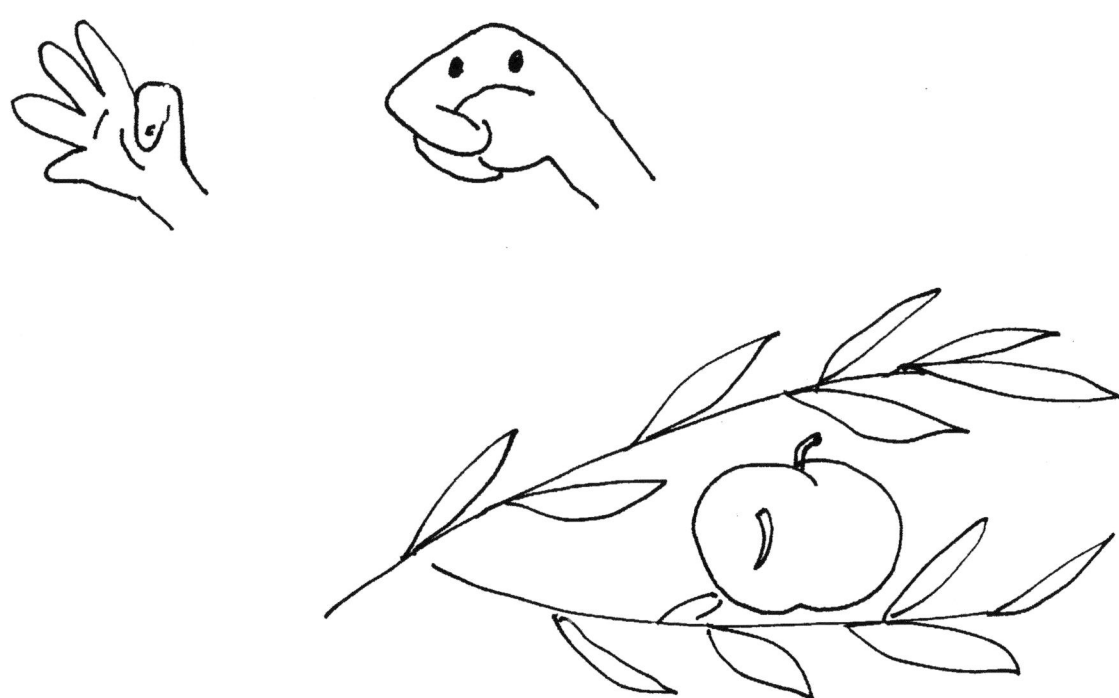

Talk About
1. What did God use to make a man? What was his name?
2. Tell about the garden God made. What was it like?
3. What did God tell Adam?

Stories From Genesis

Adam Names the Animals
Genesis 2:18-20

Materials
• small plastic animal figures or pictures of animals

While You Tell the Story
    Tell how God made animals and birds and then brought the animals to Adam for him to name. Show the animal figures or pictures to the children and let them say what they would have named that animal.

Talk About
1. Why did God make animals?
2. How did God make animals?
3. What are your favorite animals? Do you like it's name?

Stories From Genesis

Adam and Eve, Cain and Abel
Genesis 2:18-23 and 4:1, 2

Materials
- large piece of white paper
- scissors
- pen or pencil

Prepare Ahead of Time
- Fold the piece of paper accordion style into three folds so that you'll end up with four doll figures at the end of this activity.
- Optional: On the front of the paper, draw a simple outline of a person (as shown) to remind you where to cut.

While You Tell the Story

Cut out a paper doll chain as you tell about Adam. Unfold the second figure as you tell about Eve. Unfold the third as you tell about Cain. Unfold the fourth as you tell about Abel. Tell how Cain helped grow the garden; Abel helped take care of the sheep.

Talk About
1. Who were the people in our story? Who made them?
2. What did Cain do to help his family? What did Abel do to help?
3. How do you help at home? How does your family help you?

Stories From Genesis

Leaving the Garden
Genesis 3

Materials
- sand table
- figures of Adam, Eve, angel (See appendix A for suggestions.)
- twigs with leaves from trees or bushes
- red and yellow clay
- animal figures (optional)

Prepare Ahead of Time
- Put twigs in a vase or jar of water to keep them from withering.

While You Tell the Story

Make a garden in the sand by sticking the twigs into the sand as trees and placing animal figures around. Roll small balls of red clay and stick these onto one of the "trees" as fruit. Place the Adam and Eve figures in the garden, telling about how wonderful the garden was. Tell the children that Adam and Eve knew only good. They didn't know bad things. Then tell about the one tree they could not eat from, and show the tree you have put the red clay balls on. Tell how Eve looked at the tree and its fruit. It looked good. She wished she could taste it.

Then roll a small snake out of the yellow clay and place it in the tree with the fruit. Tell how the snake came and talked to Eve. He told her that the fruit would make her know good and evil and be wise like God. Show Eve picking one of the "fruits" from the tree. Show her taking it to Adam. Then tell how they began to know not only good things, but bad things. But they were still not as wise as God. The snake had lied.

Tell the rest of the story, moving the figures as needed. Place the angel figure between Adam and Eve and the garden to show how God guarded the garden so no one could come back in.

Another Idea: Make three trees on the wall using brown construction paper trunks and green poster-board tree tops. Copy and cut out different fruits from page 158 in the appendix. Attach a different color fruit to each tree. Make Adam and Eve puppets. Staple two paper plates together for each puppet. Leave space to insert your hand. Draw faces on the plates. Cut a spiral shape out of paper to make the snake. Tell the story, letting the puppets pick fruit from the trees. Attach the snake to the tree, letting him hang down.

Talk About
1. Why did Eve eat the fruit? Why did Adam eat it?
2. Did Eve obey or disobey? Did Adam obey or disobey?
3. How do you think God felt when they disobeyed? What did God do? How does God feel when we disobey?

Stories From Genesis

Noah and the Ark
Genesis 6-8

Materials
- streamers of different colors
- bulletin board and thumb tacks OR tape and blank wall
- black or gray construction paper
- masking tape
- stuffed animals of different varieties and sizes, one for each child

Prepare Ahead of Time
- Tape different colors of streamers on the wall or bulletin board to make a rainbow.
- Cut out black or gray cloud shapes and tack them over the rainbow so the rainbow is hidden.
- Make a large boat outline on the floor with masking tape.

While You Tell the Story

Have the children pretend to build an ark. Talk about how God told Noah to build the ark and Noah obeyed.

Then have all the children to get into the boat shape with their animals. Tell how Noah and his family went into the ark with the animals.

Pat gently on the floor to make the sound of rain. Rock back and forth in the boat as you tell the story. Talk about how God protected Noah during the rain and flood.

Take the clouds off the wall to reveal the rainbow at the end of the story.

Talk About
1. Have you ever ridden in a boat? What was it like?
2. Who sent the rain? Why?
3. Have you seen or heard a storm? What was it like?
4. How did God take care of the people in our story?
5. How does God take care of you?

Stories From Genesis

Tower of Babel
Genesis 11:1-9

Materials
• building blocks

While You Tell the Story

Let the children build a tower no taller than their heads. Point out how they are cooperating. Make suggestions as to how to make it sturdy and safe, with a broad base and a narrow top.

Sit around the tower to tell the story. First, tell what God told Adam when he first made him. He had said, "Have many children. . . . Fill the earth" (Genesis 1:28).

After the flood, God told Noah and his sons, "Have many children. . . . Fill the earth" (Genesis 9:1).

But there were some people who didn't want to do that. They said, "Let's build a tower. We will become famous. Then we won't be scattered over all the earth."

Talk about how people could cooperate and help each other because they all spoke the same language and could understand each other. Then, after God confused their languages, when one person was finished with his work for the day, he would say, "Adieu." Another person would say, "Adiós." Another would say, "Auf Wiedersehen!." Another would say, "Dah Sveedahneeyah."

"What does it mean? People could not understand each other. In our language it would mean "good-bye." Tell how the people stopped building the tower and scattered all over the world.

Talk About
1. Why did the people want to build the tall tower?
2. What did God do to stop them? Why couldn't the people keep working together?
3. How can you work together with other people?

Stories From Genesis

Abraham and Lot
Genesis 13:5-18

Materials
- blue bedsheet
- several pieces of green and brown construction paper
- scissors

Prepare Ahead of Time
- Cut the green construction paper in half lengthwise in a zigzag fashion to make grass.
- Cut several stone shapes from the brown construction paper.
- Stretch out the blue sheet lengthwise. Bunch up the sides to make a narrow "river."
- Place your green grass cutouts along the sides of the river.
- Scatter the stone shapes on the floor at the opposite side of the room from the river and grass.

While You Tell the Story
Walk around the room with the children and stop between the good land and bad land while you tell about the shepherds arguing. Show the children how to place their hands above their eyes as if looking far away. Look to one side of the room and then the other. Describe the different kinds of "land" you see. Ask which is the good land. Tell how Lot chose the good land.

Talk About
1. Why did Abraham and Lot want to live in different places?
2. Why did Lot choose the good land?
3. Abraham let Lot choose first. Lot chose the best for himself. Was Abraham angry?
4. What did God do for Abraham?

Stories From Genesis

Abraham and the Three Visitors
Genesis 18:1-8

Materials
- a tent or bedsheet
- bread
- cheese
- milk
- lunch meat

Prepare Ahead of Time
- Set up the tent or make one with a bedsheet draped over a table or chairs. Choose three children to be the "visitors" in the story.

While You Tell the Story
   Seat the children in a circle outside the tent. Ask the three "visitors" to stand across the room. Ask each child to hold a hand above his eyes to look far away and see the three visitors coming. Ask the visitors to come and eat. Call into the tent to ask Sarah to make some food. Reach into the tent and bring out the bread, cheese, milk, and lunch meat. Talk about how Abraham shared. Let the children eat the food.

Talk About
1. Who made the foods we eat?
2. Who ate food in our story? What did they eat? How did they get it?
3. Abraham shared food. What are some other things we can share?

Stories From Genesis

The Promise of Isaac
Genesis 18:1-15 and 21:1-7

Materials
- picture of an old woman and an old man
- tent or bedsheet
- laughing box or audio cassette/CD of someone laughing and something to play it on

Prepare Ahead of Time
- Set up the tent in the classroom or use a bedsheet draped over a table or some chairs.
- Secretly place the laughing box or cassette/CD player inside the tent, within your reach, just before the story time so it won't be discovered.

While You Tell the Story

Show the picture of the old woman and man. Ask if these people would be likely to have a baby. Talk about how very old people don't have babies of their own. Their children have grown up already.

Now tell about the old people, Abraham and Sarah, who never had any children. Tell about the three visitors who told God's promise of Isaac to Abraham. Tell how Sarah was listening in the tent. Reach into the tent and turn on the laughing box or the laughter recording. Let the children hear what Sarah's reaction was.

Then tell what God said. "Is anything too hard for the Lord?" Tell the children that the next year Sarah and Abraham did have a son. They named their son Isaac which means "he laughs."

Talk About
1. What did Sarah do when she heard she would have a baby? Why did she laugh?
2. What did God ask Sarah? Is anything too hard for God?
3. Is there something you need God to do for you? Is that too hard for God to do? How can you ask God to help you?

Stories From Genesis

Isaac Gets a Wife
Genesis 24

Materials
- poster board or corrugated cardboard
- scissors
- black construction paper
- craft sticks
- pencil
- tissue paper
- tape
- small lamp

Prepare Ahead of Time
- Make a shadow theater and shadow puppets of the servant and Rebekah. (See appendix B for instructions and patterns.)

While You Tell the Story
   Place the lamp behind the shadow theater and turn it on. Darken the room. Move the figures of the servant and Rebekah behind the screen to make shadows that the children watch as you tell the story.

Talk About
1. Why did Abraham send his servant to another country to get a wife for Isaac?
2. Why is it important to marry a good person?
3. How did the servant find out who God wanted Isaac to marry? Does God hear and answer your prayers too?

Stories From Genesis

Jacob and Esau
Genesis 25:21, 24-26

Materials
• two baby dolls

While You Tell the Story
    Ask the children to put their hand on their bellies. Tell them, "That's where the baby grows inside its mommy until it's ready to be born. Rebekah felt her baby wiggling a lot. God told her that she didn't have just one baby inside her. She had two. She was going to have twin babies. And she did. She had one baby." Hold out one baby doll. "Then, right away, she had another." Hold out another baby doll. Tell about their names and what they were like as they grew up.

Talk About
1. Have you ever seen twins? Tell about them. Were they alike or different?
2. Who was a family in our story? Who gives us our families?
3. How can we thank God for our families?

Stories From Genesis

God Talks to Isaac
Genesis 26:17-33

Materials
- star-shaped ornaments or stars made from construction paper
- string
- shallow box
- dirt or sand
- six toy figures or clothespin figures (see appendix A for story figure suggestions)
- three paper cups
- scissors
- flashlight

Prepare Ahead of Time
- Gather the star-shaped ornaments or make stars out of construction paper. Hang stars from the ceiling with string.
- Fill shallow box with dirt or sand. Cut three paper cups in half to look like wells.

While You Tell the Story
   Use the toy figures or clothespin figures, three to represent Isaac and his men, three for the other shepherds. Set each paper cup well in the dirt as you talk about the wells Isaac dug. Tell how Isaac digs wells and the enemy takes them. Finally, Isaac digs a well that the enemy doesn't take. Then make Isaac lie down. Shine a flashlight on the stars hung from the ceiling and turn down the room lights. Tell how God told Isaac, at night, not to be afraid.

Talk About
1. What was Isaac doing in our story? What happened?
2. Who took care of Isaac? What did God tell him?
3. Does God take care of you at night? How?

Stories From Genesis

Jacob Deceives Isaac
Genesis 27

Materials
- cotton or polyester quilt batting (used for making quilts and stuffed toys)

While You Tell the Story

Talk about how people look different. Even brothers and sisters are sometimes very different. Talk about what made Esau and Jacob different. Tell about how Isaac sent Esau out to hunt for food for his dinner, and how Rebekah made plans for Jacob to get the blessing instead.

Let the children feel the cotton or batting. Tell how hairy Esau was. Then have the children close their eyes. Ask them to pretend they are Isaac. Lay the batting over your hand and arm. Tell the children you are Esau. Let them feel your hand. Ask, "Do I feel like smooth Jacob or hairy Esau?"

Let the children open their eyes and guess what they think happened next. Finish telling the story.

Talk About
1. Why did Jacob lie to Isaac?
2. How did the lie make Esau feel? How did it make Isaac feel? What did Jacob have to do then?
3. What is a lie? Why is it wrong to lie?

Stories From Genesis

Jacob's Dream
Genesis 28:10-17

Materials
- white plastic spoons, one for each child
- a black permanent marker
- one piece of plain white paper for each child
- transparent tape
- newspaper
- large paper bag
- stapler

Prepare Ahead of Time
- Stuff crumpled newspaper into the paper bag to make a rock. Staple or tape the end of the bag closed.
- Let the children make angel puppets by drawing a face on the bowl of the spoon with the marker. Fold the white paper accordion-style. Tape the center of the folded paper to the center of the spoon to make wings.

While You Tell the Story
    Choose one child to lay his head on the rock and pretend to be Jacob dreaming. Tell the story. Let the children fly their puppet angels around Jacob.

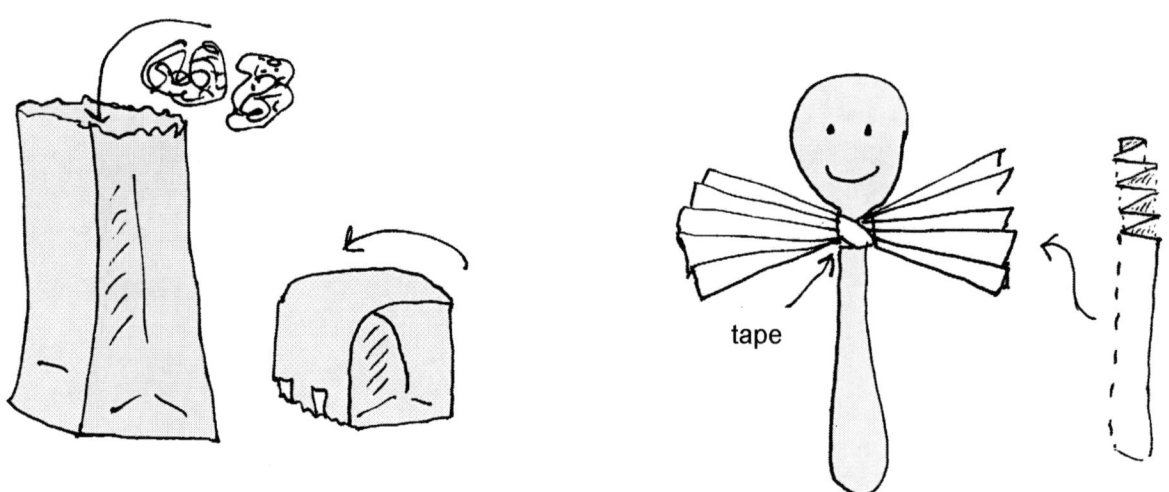

Talk About
1. What did Jacob do when he got tired?
2. What did Jacob see in his dream? What did God tell him? How did Jacob feel after that?
3. Are there times when you feel all alone? Are you ever all alone? Who is with you?

Stories From Genesis

Rachel's Sheep
Genesis 29:1-12

Materials
- empty cardboard box (to represent a well)
- pillow large enough to fit over the opening of the box (to represent a large rock)

While You Tell the Story

Place the box "well" on one side of the room. Put the pillow "rock" on top of the well to cover the opening of the "well." Explain to the children what a well is.

Divide the children into three groups. Ask one child to be the shepherd for each group. The other children are sheep. Put two groups by the well. Put the third group across the room. Their shepherd is Rachel.

Choose a child to be Jacob. Tell the story, guiding the children to move as you tell about how Jacob travels and talks to shepherds watching sheep by a covered well. Tell how Rachel comes with her sheep to the well. Tell how Jacob takes the cover off the well and all the sheep get to drink water.

Talk About
1. Have you ever seen sheep before? What are they like?
2. What is the person called who takes care of sheep? (Shepherd)
3. How does a shepherd take care of sheep? Was the shepherd being kind to the sheep?
4. Do you have any pets? (Or your grandmother or neighbor?) Who takes care of them? How can you be kind to your pets?

Stories From Genesis

Joseph's Colorful Coat
Genesis 37:1-3

Materials
- a solid color man's shirt or pillowcase
- fabric markers

Prepare Ahead of Time
- If you use a pillowcase, cut a head hole at the end opposite the opening. Cut an opening down the center front. Then cut arm holes on each side.

While You Tell the Story

Seat the children in a circle. Holding the coat, walk around on the outside of the circle. Touch each child's head as you pass. Say, "Joseph was a young man who had eleven brothers. Joseph's daddy loved him and gave him a coat."

The child whose head you touch as you said "coat" stands up. Put the coat on him. Then he walks around the circle, repeating what you said, touching another child who stands and puts on the coat. Continue as long as interest lasts.

FOR PILLOWCASE "COAT"

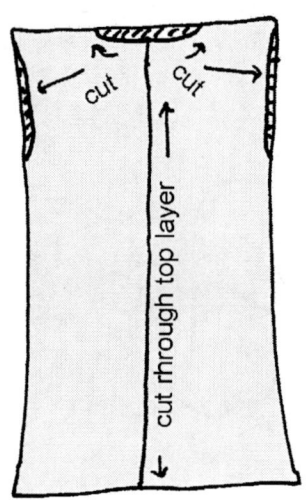

Color the coat with fabric markers, OR let the children help color it.

Talk About
1. When do people give gifts?
2. How do you feel when someone gives you a gift? How do people feel when you give them gifts?
3. Who gave a gift in the story? What did he give? Why?

Stories From Genesis

Joseph's Dreams
Genesis 37:1-11

Materials
- yellow construction paper
- drinking straws
- scissors
- tape

Prepare Ahead of Time
- From construction paper, cut out a sun, a moon, some stars, and grain sheaths from patterns on page 159 in the appendix. Tape them as shown to drinking straws. Each child will need one straw figure (sun, moon, stars, or grain).

While You Tell the Story
Give each child one straw figure. As you tell the story, the children can use the figures as puppets to bow down at the appropriate times.

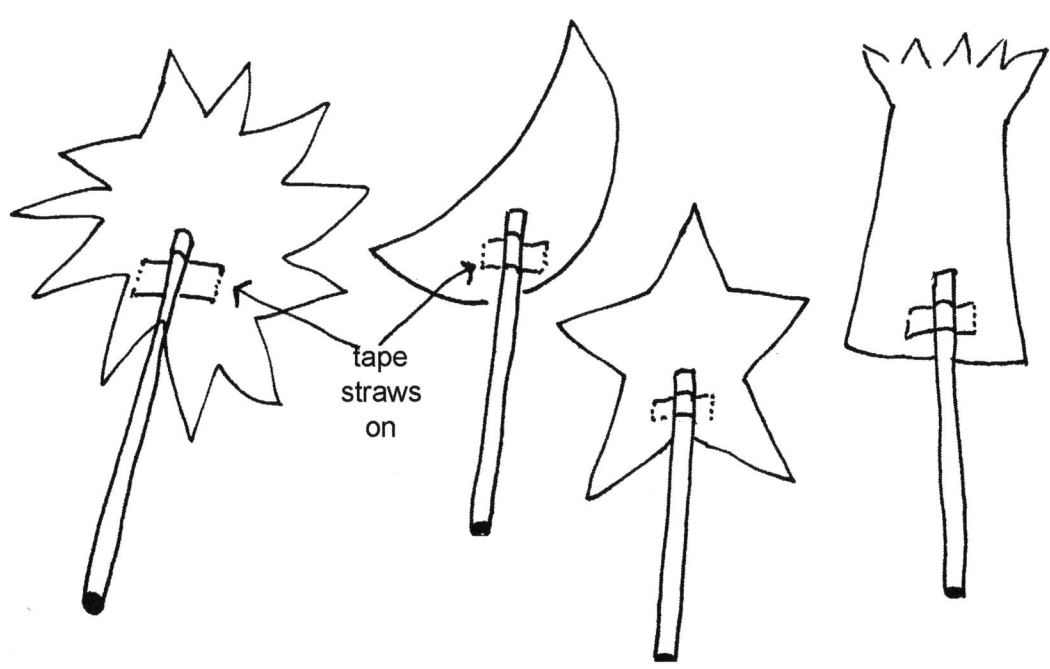

tape straws on

Talk About
1. What did Joseph dream?
2. How did Joseph's family feel when they heard about his dreams? (Joseph's brothers made fun of him. They were jealous. They wanted to be the most important.)
3. How do you think Joseph felt? Why does God want us to be kind to others instead of making fun of them?

Stories From Genesis

Joseph at Potiphar's House
Genesis 39:1-6

Materials
• assortment of household tools (brooms, stirring spoon, dusting cloths, kitchen towel, etc.)

While You Tell the Story

Tell how Joseph lives and works at Potiphar's house. Tell how Joseph does a good job of taking care of the house. Tell how Potiphar puts Joseph in charge of everything he has.

Let each child take a turn holding one of the household tools. As a child pretends to use a tool, sing about Joseph's work to the tune of "The Mulberry Bush."

For a broom, sing,

This is the way that Joseph swept,
Joseph swept, Joseph swept.
This is the way that Joseph swept.
He took care of Potiphar's house.

Substitute other tools: stirred (dinner), dusted (tables), dried (dishes)

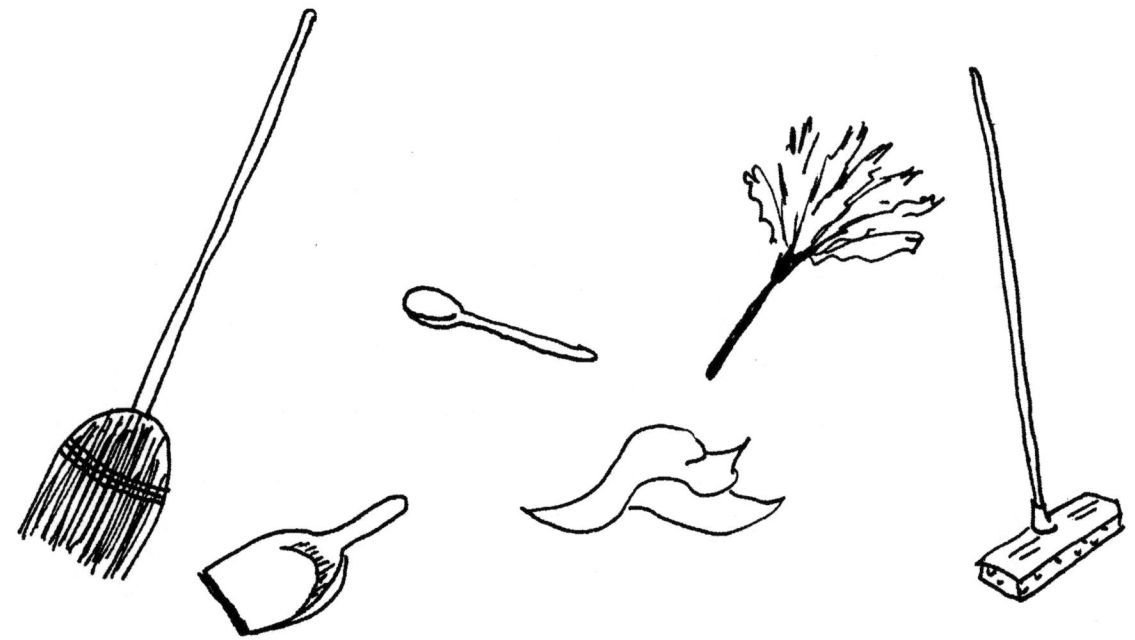

Talk About
1. Who took care of the place in our story? What did he do?
2. God wants us to take care of the things he's give us. How do you take care of your room at home?
3. How do you help take care of the place where you live?
4. What are some ways you help take care of our classroom?

Stories From Genesis

More Dreams
Genesis 40, 41

Materials
- chalkboard
- colored chalk, eraser

While You Tell the Story

As you tell the story, draw or let the children draw on the chalkboard the items mentioned in the story (the cup of the cupbearer, the grain of Pharaoh's dream, and the cows–seven fat, seven thin). Try the simple suggestions on this page.

Talk About
1. Why do you think God sent these dreams to Pharaoh? How did Joseph know what the dreams meant?
2. Joseph obeyed God and prayed to God. God made Joseph wise. Can God make you wise too? How?
3. Joseph had hard times in jail, but God made everything turn out all right. What kind of hard times do you have? Who can make it turn out all right?

Stories From Genesis

Joseph's Silver Cup
Genesis 44:1 – 45:14

Materials
- one disposable plastic cup
- aluminum foil
- two paper lunch sacks

Prepare Ahead of Time
- Open up the paper sacks.
- Cover the cup with the foil by folding the foil around and into the cup. Place the foil-covered cup into only one of the sacks. Close the tops of both sacks by folding them over.

While You Tell the Story

Set a paper sack in front of each child. Take note of which child gets the sack with the cup in it. Tell the children to pretend to be Joseph's brothers. Ask them not to touch the sacks. Tell them what Joseph did. Then pretend to be the Egyptian looking for the cup. Go to each child at random and ask, "Did you take the cup?" Then open the sack and turn it upside down. Nothing falls out. Go to the child with the cup last. Finish telling what happened and how Joseph told his brothers who he was.

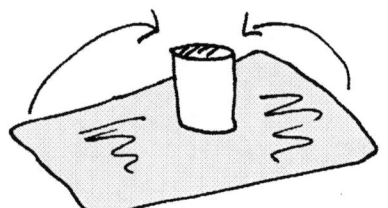   

Talk About
1. Why didn't Joseph's brothers know who he was?
2. Why did Joseph put the cup in his brother's sack? How do you think Benjamin felt when he saw the cup in his sack?
3. Joseph could have been very angry at his brothers. They were the ones who sent him away. But Joseph forgave his brothers. How do you think they felt then? Are you angry at anyone? How can you forgive him?

Egypt to the Promised Land

Baby Moses
Exodus 1, 2

Materials
- sandbox
- foil
- reeds cut from green construction paper as shown
- clothespin or toy figures of a girl and a woman (See appendix A for suggestions.)
- clay
- plastic bottle cap for a basket

Prepare Ahead of Time
- Cut out the reeds from green paper. Fold and wrinkle the foil in a long strip to make a river. Put it across the sand in the sandbox. Stand the reeds along the side of the river.

While You Tell the Story
    Begin telling the story, "Once there was a baby born to a family who loved God. But they lived in Egypt where there was a mean king."

    As you tell this part, begin shaping a small baby out of clay. Two small circles, one on the other like a snowman, will be sufficient. Make this figure small enough to fit into the bottle cap basket.

    As you tell the rest of the story, place the basket into the river, and move the other figures in place as the story requires.

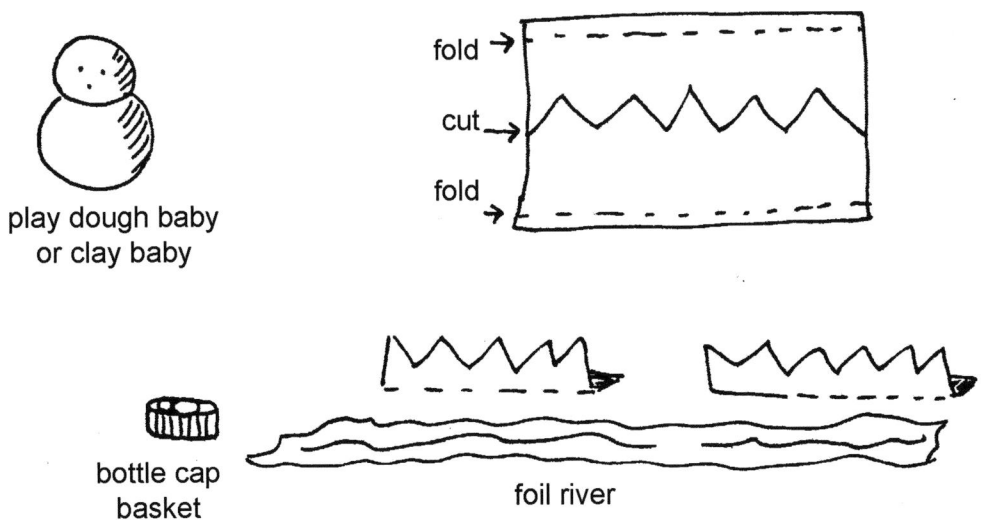

play dough baby or clay baby

bottle cap basket

foil river

Talk About
1. Why did Moses' mother put him in a basket in the river?
2. How did Miriam help? Who else was watching over the baby?
3. How can you be a helper?

Egypt to the Promised Land

Burning Bush
Exodus 3, 4

Materials
- leaves cut out of green construction paper
- glue
- flames cut out of red, orange, and yellow construction paper
- double-sided tape or sticky temporary adhesive (like Plasti-Tak)
- toy snake
- one piece of white poster board
- long stick for Moses' rod

Prepare Ahead of Time
- Cut out leaves and flames according to the patterns on page 160 in the appendix. Glue the leaves onto the poster board in the shape of a bush. (The children may glue the leaves onto the bush in class as a separate activity, if you like.)

While You Tell the Story
   Place the bush poster on a wall or bulletin board. As you tell the story, hold the rod and let the children stick the flames onto the bush using the double-sided tape or other adhesive. Tell how the bush was burning, but not burning up. Tell how God spoke to Moses from the bush and what he said. Throw down the rod. Then throw the snake next to it and tell how the road became a snake. Then pick up the snake and rod. Put the snake away. Tell the rest of the story.

Talk About
1. What did God want Moses to do?
2. How did Moses feel about what God told him to do?
3. God showed Moses that he would be with Moses and help him. When is God with you? How does God help you?

Egypt to the Promised Land

The Plagues in Egypt
Exodus 7-11

Materials
- four transparent plastic jars with lids
- water
- red flood coloring
- rock salt
- black and brown construction paper
- hole punch
- scissors
- baby powder
- toy cow, frog, and insect (locust-type) figures

Prepare Ahead of Time
- Pour water into one of the jars until the jar is about half full. Mix a couple of drops of red food coloring in the water. This jar represents the blood. For hail, pour some rock salt into a second jar. For gnats, punch several holes in the black paper with the hole punch. You will need a small handful of the black circles you punched out. Put them in the third jar. For flies, cut out small brown paper triangles. Put them in a jar.
- If necessary, make a clothespin cow with the pattern on page 161 in the appendix. Cut out 3-inch green circles for frogs and 3-inch black triangles for locusts. Fold the triangles in half to make winged locusts.

While You Tell the Story
Tell how God sent Moses to Pharaoh. Each time, say that Moses said, "Let my people go." But Pharaoh would not. So God sent the next plague. As you tell about the ten plagues, follow the instructions on page 161 in the appendix.

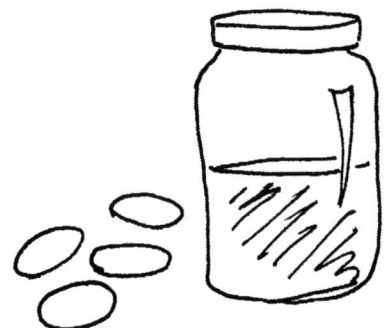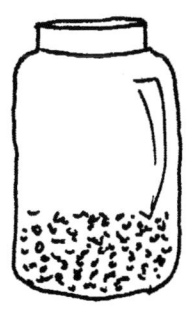

Talk About
1. Why did God do all of those wonders in Egypt? God said one reason was so "you may know that I am the Lord." Is there another reason?
2. Could anyone else make all those things happen? We see some of God's wonders every day–like lightning and thunder–but we see them so often we forget that they show God's power.
3. What else shows God's power? (Changing leaves, wind, babies, plants growing.) Let's watch for God's wonders and thank him when we see them.

Egypt to the Promised Land

Crossing the Red Sea
Exodus 13:17 – 14:31

Materials
- two blue bedsheets
- one piece of white poster board
- white cotton or polyester quilt batting (optional)
- glue
- flashlight
- one piece of orange poster board
- scissors
- broom handle or long dowel
- masking tape

Prepare Ahead of Time
• Cut out a large cloud shape from the white and orange poster board. To the white side, tape the dowel or broom handle as shown. Glue the clouds together, so there is a white cloud on one side and an orange cloud on the other. Optional: glue the batting or fiberfill over the white side.

While You Tell the Story
  Place the sheets side by side on the floor. Bunch them up so that they have "waves" in them. Pretend to be the Israelites leaving Egypt, with Pharaoh's army coming close behind. Come to the sea and discuss how you could get across.
  Have one child carry the cloud. Tell how it led the people–the cloud by day and the fire by night. When they "camp" at night, shine a flashlight on the orange side of the cloud. Turn the room lights off and let the children "sleep" on the floor. Tell how the cloud came between Pharaoh's army and God's people when they were camped by the sea.
  Then the sea rolled back. Pull the two sheets apart, and let the children walk between the sheets "on dry ground."

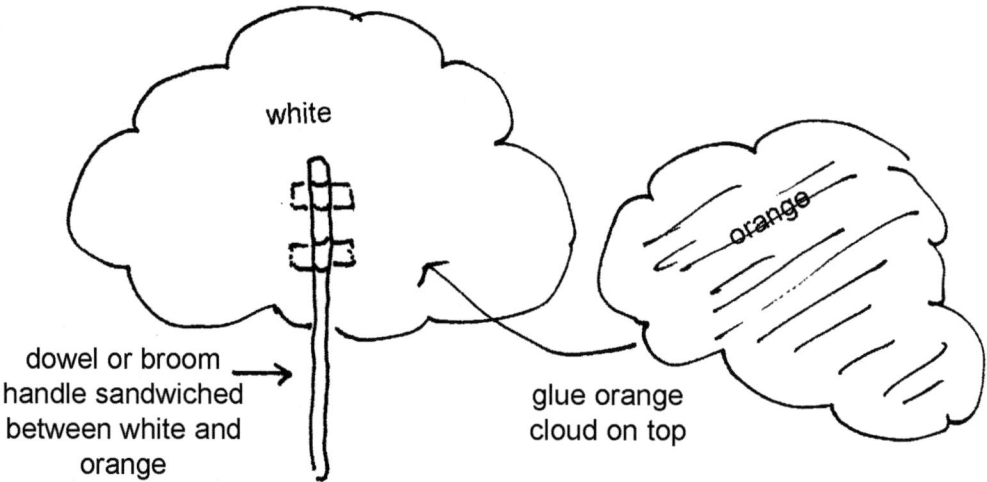

Talk About
1. How do you think the people felt when they found out that the enemy army was chasing them?
2. What happened when the people came to the sea?
3. How did God take care of his people? How does God take care of you?

Egypt to the Promised Land

Israelites Praise God After Crossing the Red Sea
Exodus 14; 15:1-21

Materials
- two blue bedsheets

While You Tell the Story

Place the sheets side by side on the floor. Bunch them up so that they have "waves" in them. Pretend to be the Israelites leaving Egypt, with Pharaoh's army coming close behind. Come to the sea and discuss how you could get across. Show how Moses held his hand out. Let everyone make a wind sound. Pull each sheet back so there's a path in the sea. Everyone walks across. Then praise God, saying some of the things that the story in Exodus tells us they said. Or you may read part of the passage. Clap and praise God.

Talk About
1. How do you think the people felt when they found out that the enemy army was chasing them?
2. What happened when the people came to the sea?
3. Who praised God in our story? What did they do?
4. When can you praise God? Where can we praise God? How can we praise God?

> Egypt to the Promised Land

Bitter Water Turns Sweet
Exodus 15:22-27

Materials
- salt
- water
- two pitchers
- paper cups

Prepare Ahead of Time
- Mix salt in a pitcher of water. Have fresh water available.

While You Tell the Story

Walk around the room with the children, pretending you are the people in the story. Tell how God's people walked for three days and could not find water. Pretend to get thirsty and look for water. Get thirstier and thirstier. Finally, say you've found water! Everyone sits down.

Pour a taste of the salty water for each child. Tell the children how the people in the story found water but it was bitter and they couldn't drink it. After telling what God did, pour fresh water for everyone to drink.

> **Talk About**
> 1. What were the people in our story looking for? What did they find? What did they say?
> 2. What did Moses do? Who made the water good to drink?
> 3. Did you like the bitter water? Why?
> 4. Who gives you good water to drink?

Egypt to the Promised Land

Manna and Quail
Exodus 16

Materials
- bedsheet or tablecloth
- oyster crackers
- blocks and flashlight (optional)

While You Tell the Story

Spread the sheet or tablecloth on the floor. The children should pretend to be God's people in the wilderness. Tell them how the people complained that there was not enough food. Tell them how Moses talked to God about it. Then tell them to pretend to go to sleep at night around the tablecloth or sheet.

While their eyes are closed, place the oyster crackers all over the tablecloth or sheet. Turn the lights back on and tell the children to wake up and see what the Lord sent. Then talk about how God also sent quail (a type of bird) for their meat sometimes. Have the children gather and eat the "manna" crackers, making sure everyone gets some.

Optional: Use the building blocks to build a "campfire" around a flashlight. As the children pretend to sleep, turn out the lights and turn on the flashlight. Turn the room lights back on when it's "morning."

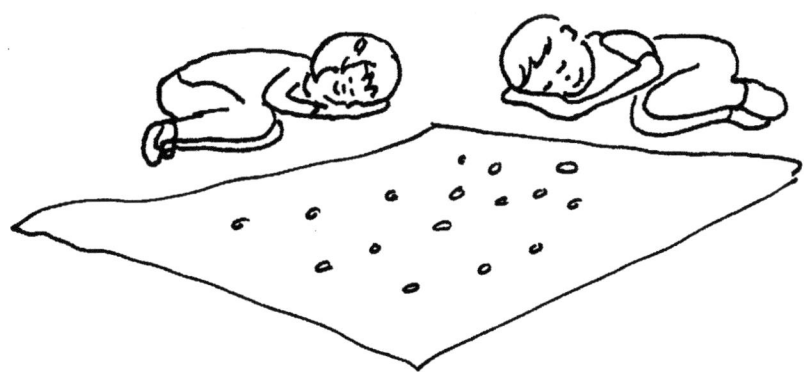

Talk About
1. Who gives us food to eat? What are your favorite foods?
2. Who ate food in our story? What kind of food did they eat? How did they get it?

> Egypt to the Promised Land

The Ten Commandments
Exodus 19, 20

Materials
- play dough
- craft sticks

Prepare Ahead of Time
- If you need to make play dough, mix together 3 parts flour, 1 part salt, and 1 part water.

While You Tell the Story
　　As you tell the story, make tablets out of the dough. Let the children pretend to write the laws on the tablets using the craft sticks as writing instruments. As you tell the laws, you may want to say them in words a young child can understand:

1. No other gods.
2. No idols.
3. No bad words.
4. Remember the worship day.
5. Obey your father and mother.
6. No killing.
7. Stay with the one you're married to.
8. No stealing.
9. No lying.
10. No jealousy (getting angry because you can't have what someone else has).

Another Idea: Put a chair on a table and drape a dark sheet over the chair and table. Sit around this "mountain" to tell the story. Let a child turn the lights on and off to make lightning. Have the children drum their hands on the floor to make thunder. Make the play dough tablets and review the commandments.

> **Talk About**
> 1. Why did God give rules to his people?
> 2. Can we follow these rules too?
> 3. What happens when we disobey God?

Egypt to the Promised Land

Building the Tabernacle
Exodus 35:30 – 36:2

Materials
- blocks
- unbreakable plate
- aluminum foil
- inexpensive jewelry or marbles
- blocks of wood
- toy hammers
- fabrics swatches

While You Tell the Story

Seat the children in a circle around a pile of blocks. Tell the children that God wanted his people to build a worship house. Many people helped. God gave each person different skills to help.

Give one child a plate covered with aluminum foil. He works with silver and gold. Give another child some jewelry or pretty marbles. He works with jewels. Give blocks of wood to wood carvers, toy hammers to carpenters, and fabric to the weavers. Tell how they helped each other build. Let the children build with the blocks.

Talk About
1. Who helped in our story? What did God want them to do?
2. How did they help? Who gave the people their skills to help?
3. How can you help at home? How can you help in class?

Egypt to the Promised Land

Twelve Spies
Numbers 13 – 14:9

Materials
- twelve figures of men (see appendix A for suggestions)

While You Tell the Story

Let the children count the figures. Tell about the twelve men who were chosen by Moses to be spies and go into the new land to find out about it. They were supposed to find out what kind of people lived there, what kinds of crops they grew, and what kind of cities they had. God wanted to give this land to his people. Ask the children to sit on the floor and bend their knees to form mountains. Make the spies walk over the mountains and look down in the valleys to see what the land is like. Then bring them back to where they started. Tell what the report was. Set two of the figures aside. Ask the children to count the ten and then the two. Tell what God said when the people decided to believe the ten spies who thought they could not take the land (verses 11-12).

Talk About
1. Why did the ten spies say they could not take the land? What had God told them?
2. What did the two spies, Joshua and Caleb, say?
3. Did the ten spies believe God or did the two spies believe God? Can you think of great things that God has done that shows that he "can do all things" (Job 42:2)?

Egypt to the Promised Land

Aaron's Staff Blooms
Numbers 17

Materials
- twelve sticks or dowels
- white tissue paper
- black permanent marker
- double-sided tape
- bedsheet or tent

Prepare Ahead of Time
• Cut small squares of white tissue paper and crumple them to make flowers. Put tape at various places around one stick or dowel.
• Set up the tent in the classroom or make one by draping a sheet across some chairs.
• Just before story time, pour the crumpled tissue flowers in a pile on the floor inside the tent.

While You Tell the Story
Sit outside the tent to tell the story. Show the twelve sticks. Write Aaron's name on the one with the tape. Then place the sticks in the tent. Place Aaron's stick on the pile of tissue paper and roll it around so the paper sticks onto the tape. Ask the children to pretend to sleep. Then wake up and check the sticks. See whose stick budded.

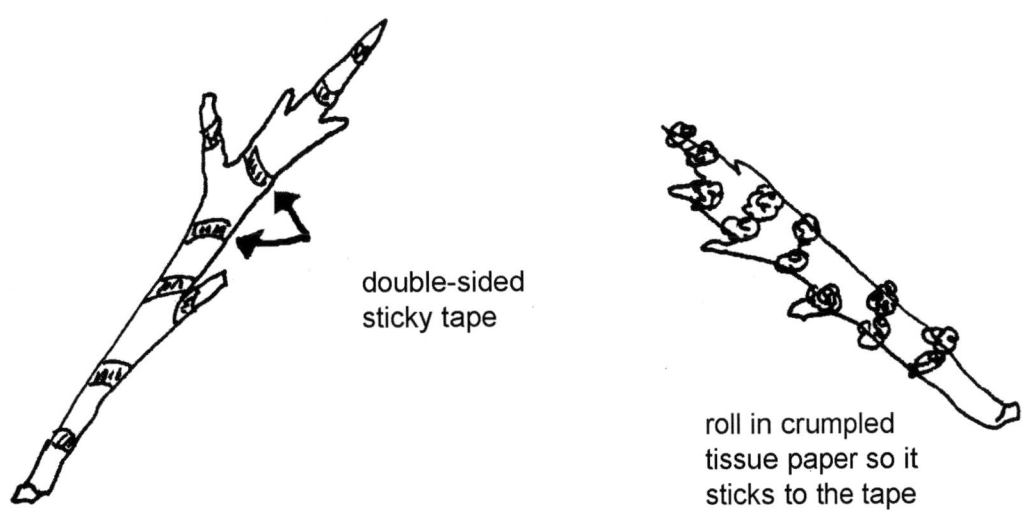

double-sided sticky tape

roll in crumpled tissue paper so it sticks to the tape

Talk About
1. Why were the people complaining about Aaron?
2. How did God show the people which man was supposed to lead them?
3. How do we feel when we complain? How do other people feel? Does God want us to complain? Why not?

Egypt to the Promised Land

Balaam's Talking Donkey
Numbers 22

Materials
- blocks
- small toy figures: one donkey or horse, two people to be Balaam and the king, and one angel (See appendix A for suggestions.)

While You Tell the Story

Let the children make a road by lining up blocks across the floor, end-to-end. Stand a few blocks up sideways to make a wall next to the road at one place. Tell the story by showing the figures traveling down the road. Set the angel in the way at the appropriate times.

If you want to continue the story, you can tell how the king took Balaam up on three different mountains, hoping that perhaps on one of them Balaam would curse God's people. Use the children as mountains, placing the figures on their knees, shoulders, or heads when the king and Balaam are on the mountains.

Talk About
1. Who saw the angel that God sent? What did the donkey do? What did Balaam do?
2. Do you suppose that God wanted to make sure that Balaam would bless God's people and tell the good things that God would do for them?
3. When Balaam saw the angel, he decided he would be sure to obey God. What are some ways you can you obey God?

Egypt to the Promised Land

Jericho's Walls Fall Down
Joshua 2; 6:1 – 25

Materials
- blocks
- tablecloth or bedsheet
- piece of red yarn

While You Tell the Story

Spread the tablecloth or sheet on the floor. Let the children build a city with blocks on top of the tablecloth or sheet. Since most cities today don't have walls, you may need to explain why there were walls around the cities. Then tell the story. When you tell about Rahab, place the red yarn in between two blocks in the wall so that it hangs down. March with the children around the tablecloth seven times. Pretend to blow trumpets. Shout. While you hold Rahab's house secure, instruct the children to tug on the sides of the tablecloth to make the walls fall. Tell how Rahab's house didn't fall. She and her family were safe.

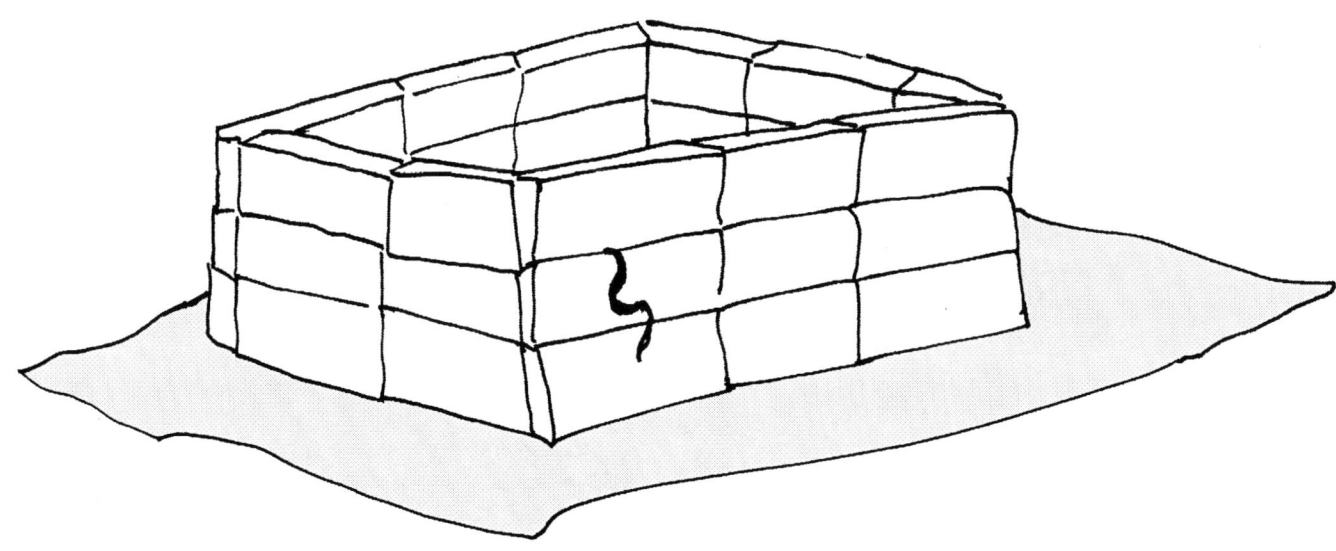

Talk About
1. The enemies were inside the city. They didn't love or obey God. What was Rahab like?
2. Most armies would have to fight the enemy to take the city. How did God's people win over Jericho?
3. What did the spies promise Rahab? Did they keep their promise? Why is it good to keep your promises?

Egypt to the Promised Land

The Sun Stands Still
Joshua 10:1–15

Materials
- yellow balloon
- dowel rod or drinking straw
- string

Prepare Ahead of Time
- Inflate the balloon. Tie it onto the dowel or drinking straw.

While You Tell the Story
  Choose one child to be the sun. Guide him across the room as he holds the balloon high to show how the sun usually goes across the sky each day. Then tell about the battle. Guide the child across the room again. This time, stop when Joshua says, "Sun, stand still." Tell about how God's people won the fight. Repeat the story as a game, letting the children take turns being the sun and being Joshua who tells the sun to stand still.

Talk About
1. Why did Joshua want the sun to stay still in the sky?
2. Who made the sun? Who is in charge of the sun? Did Joshua make the sun stand still or did God?
3. What can you see around us that shows God's power?

Egypt to the Promised Land

Deborah
Judges 4:1-16

Materials
- umbrella
- safety pins
- markers
- large pieces of green construction paper
- cardboard box large enough for a child to sit in

Prepare Ahead of Time
- Cut out long palm tree leaves from the green construction paper using the pattern on page 162 in the appendix. Safety pin them to the umbrella, making a palm tree.
- With markers, draw one wheel on each side of the large box, and make chariot designs on the box.

While You Tell the Story
Choose one child to be Deborah. She may sit under "the Palm of Deborah," holding the handle of the umbrella. Choose one child to ride in the chariot to represent the enemy army. Choose one child to be Barak. Tell how Deborah called Barak and gave him a message from God, but Barak would not go unless Deborah went with him. Tell how Deborah went, and the enemy army was confused. Give the children rides in the chariot, reviewing the story.

Talk About
1. What message did God ask Deborah to give to Barak?
2. Why do you think Barak didn't want to go without Deborah?
3. Deborah was brave and God let her help win the fight over the enemies. When do you need to be brave? Who can help you?

Egypt to the Promised Land

Gideon and the Fleece
Judges 6:36-40

Materials
- cotton or polyester quilt batting (filler material for quilts and pillows)
- two Styrofoam plates
- water
- bowl

Prepare Ahead of Time
- Divide the batting into two parts. Each part should be the size to fit onto a Styrofoam plate.

While You Tell the Story
Show the children a dry piece of batting as you tell about what Gideon asked God. Place the batting on a plate. Ask the children to pretend to go to sleep. When their eyes are closed, sprinkle water all over the batting. Ask the children to wake up. Let them feel the wet batting. Then show another piece of dry batting. Tell what Gideon asked God to do. Ask the children to sleep again. While their eyes are closed, sprinkle droplets of water on the edges of the plate, but not on the batting. Then ask the children to wake up and see and feel the dry batting and wet plate.

Talk About
1. Why did Gideon put the wool out that night?
2. Did God hear Gideon's prayer? Did God answer Gideon?
3. Does God hear you when you pray? Does God answer you?

Egypt to the Promised Land

Gideon's Men
Judges 7:1-8

Materials
- blue bedsheet

While You Tell the Story

Stretch out the sheet so that it is long and narrow like a river with little waves in it. Ask all of the children to march around with you pretending to be Gideon's men. Tell the story. Tell about the scared men who went home. Ask the children to drink water from the river. Show them the two different ways to drink. Tell about the other men who went home. Tell them why God left Gideon with only a few men. God said, "I don't want them to brag that they saved themselves."

Talk About
1. Why didn't God let Gideon have a big army with lots of men?
2. How do you think Gideon felt when he had only a few men?
3. What does it mean to brag? There are many things you can do, but who made you able to do those things?

Egypt to the Promised Land

Gideon and the Torches
Judges 7:8-22

Materials
- piece of construction paper
- stapler
- flashlight
- plastic pitcher

Prepare Ahead of Time
- Roll the piece of construction paper into a cone, as shown, to represent a horn. Staple it together.
- Put the flashlight into the pitcher.

While You Tell the Story

Seat the children in a circle. Pretend to be Gideon's men around the enemy camp at night. Turn off the classroom light, and turn on the flashlight inside the pitcher. Tell how Gideon and his men blew their trumpets. Pretend to blow the paper trumpet. Let the children pretend to blow trumpets. Tell how Gideon smashed his pitcher and held his torch high, shouting, "A sword for the Lord and for Gideon!"

Remove the pitcher from the flashlight, letting the light shine. Let the children pretend to smash a pitcher and hold a torch high, shouting, "A sword for the Lord and for Gideon!" Tell what happened to the enemy.

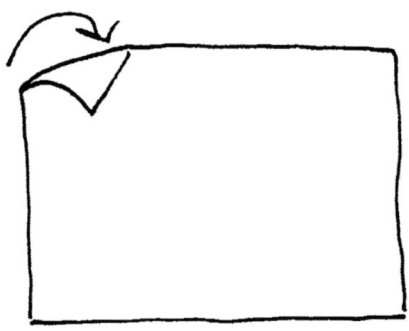 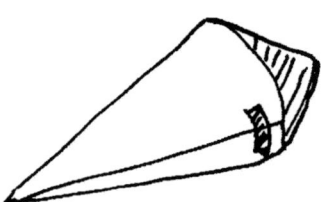

Talk About
1. How would you feel if you were Gideon at night watching the enemy camp?
2. How could Gideon be brave?
3. Gideon trusted God to take care of him. Did God take care of Gideon?
4. Can you trust God to take care of you? Tell about a time when God took care of you.

Egypt to the Promised Land

Samson and Delilah
Judges 16:1-21

Materials
- one Barbie doll, one Ken doll (or similar dolls)
- old pillowcase, bedsheet, or other fabric
- small gift box (the size jewelry comes in)
- seven 6-inch lengths of string
- one 6-inch length of yarn
- scissors
- rubber band
- brown or black yarn
- blocks

Prepare Ahead of Time
• Make clothes for the dolls by cutting a piece of fabric about 8 by 8 inches for the woman doll and 5 by 8 inches for the man doll. Cut arm holes in the pieces of fabric and slip them onto the dolls. Cut strips of fabric ? by 9 inches to tie around the fabric as belts to hold on the clothes.
• Make long hair for the man doll by tying 6-inch lengths of yarn onto the rubber band as shown on page 163 in the appendix. Then slip it onto the doll's head.

While You Tell the Story
Have the children build two columns of blocks about 8 inches apart. Tell the story, showing Samson asleep as Delilah places the seven pieces of string across him. Show him jumping up and shaking the string off. Do the same with the yarn.

Then use the small box to represent the loom. As Samson sleeps the third time, put the ends of Samson's hair into the box and snap the lid on.

Show Samson waking up and shaking the loom off. Then show Samson sleeping and Delilah cutting his hair. Take the rubber band off the doll's head. Tell the rest of the story. Finally, have the Samson doll knock over the columns to conquer the enemy.

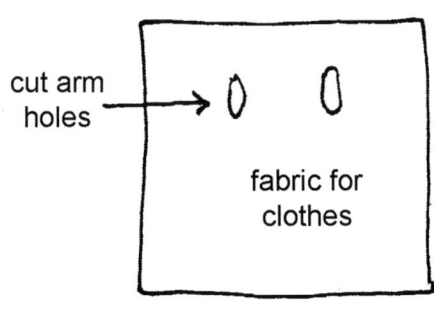

Talk About
1. What kind of friend was Delilah?
2. Why is it important to choose good friends?
3. What kind of person makes a good friend? How can you be a good friend?

43

Egypt to the Promised Land

Ruth
The Book of Ruth

Materials
- four figures—one man, three women (See appendix A for suggestions.)
- dry grass
- string
- scissors

Prepare Ahead of Time
- Make little bundles of the dry grass, tying them with string.

While You Tell the Story

Tell how Naomi told Ruth and Orpah she was moving back to Judah. (Use the appropriate figures.) Show how Orpah went home, but Ruth insisted on going with Naomi.

Tell how Ruth helped Naomi by gathering the grain. Using bundles of dry grass, pull out a little from each bundle to show how the harvesters would leave whatever fell out of the bundle for the poor people to gather. Show how Ruth gathered the grain.

Tell how Boaz saw Ruth, met her, and later married her.

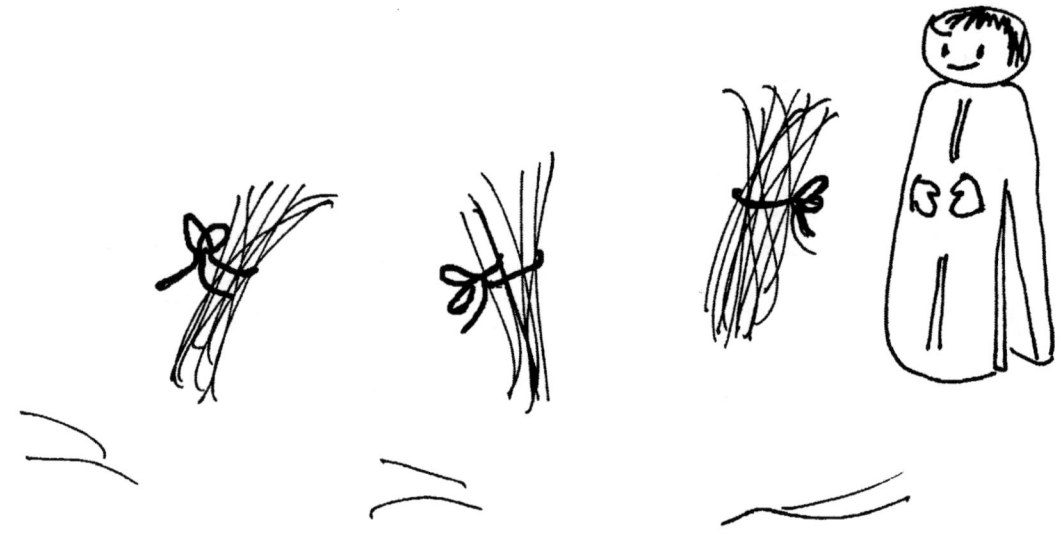

Talk About
1. How did Ruth feel about Naomi?
2. Why did Ruth go out to gather grain? Why didn't Naomi go?
3. Ruth was helping Naomi. How can you help your family?

Egypt to the Promised Land

Hannah and Samuel
1 Samuel 1–2:11

Materials
- four paper plates
- gray yarn
- markers
- stapler
- one 10-inch square of cloth
- glue

Prepare Ahead of Time
• Make puppets out of the paper plates as shown. Staple two paper plates together leaving a space open at the bottom so your hand can fit through. Make two puppets this way.
• For the Hannah puppet, draw a happy face on one side and a sad face on the other. Attach the cloth as a head scarf by stapling it at the top.

While You Tell the Story
Tell the story using the sad-faced Hannah puppet first. Put it on one hand. On the other hand, put the Eli puppet and tell what happened when they met.
Then take the puppets off and tell about the birth of Samuel.
Meanwhile, move the scarf to cover the sad face, and turn the Hannah puppet around so the happy face shows. Tell how thankful Hannah was, and how she kept her promise to God.

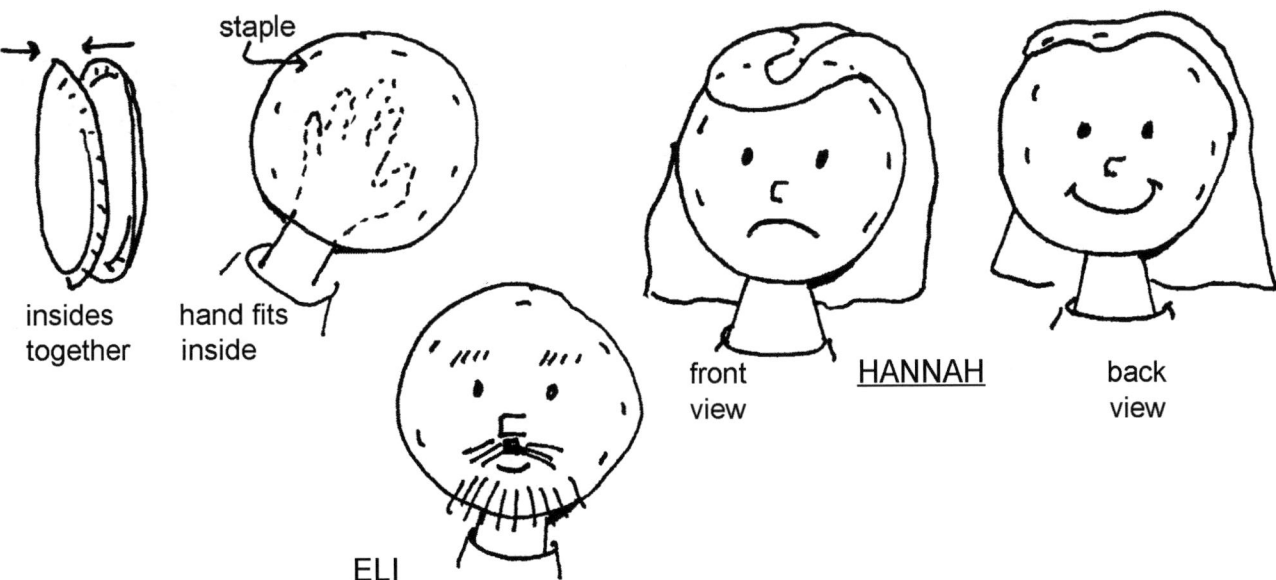

Talk About
1. Who did Hannah talk to when she was very sad?
2. Can you talk to God when you are happy? What is another time when you can talk to God?
3. God heard Hannah. He answered her prayer. Does God hear your prayers too? Does God answer your prayers?

Egypt to the Promised Land

Samuel's New Coats
1 Samuel 2:18-21

Materials
- three or four dolls of different sizes with shirts to fit each doll

While You Tell the Story

Tell how Hannah took Samuel to live with and help Eli.

Show the smallest doll. Tell how Samuel grew. Show a doll larger than the first one. Tell how Hannah made new clothes for Samuel, because he had grown. Put that doll's shirt on it. Show a doll larger than the second one. Tell how the next year Hannah made more new clothes, because Samuel was still growing. Put that doll's shirt on it. Do this again with the largest doll.

Tell how Samuel grew up serving God.

Talk About
1. Which people in your family are smaller than you? Which people are bigger than you?
2. You were smaller one time. What happened? What happens to your clothes when you grow bigger?
3. Samuel was still growing. Was he able to help even though he was little?
4. You're still growing. How can you help at home? How can you help in our classroom?

Samuel Hears God

Samuel Hears God
1 Samuel 3

Materials
- none

While You Tell the Story

Tell about the boy Samuel helping old Eli at the worship place. Tell how Samuel went to bed one night. Ask the children to put their heads on their hands and close their eyes as if they were asleep. Tell about God calling, "Samuel, Samuel." Have the children wake up and say to Eli, "Here I am." Explain that Eli said, "I did not call. Go back to sleep." Have the children put their heads on their hands and sleep again. They wake up again when God calls. They go back to sleep again when Eli says to. Then wake up again when God calls. Then Eli says that next time Samuel should answer, "Speak, Lord, I'm listening." The children go to sleep again. Call, "Samuel, Samuel" again. The children say what Eli told Samuel to say: "Speak, Lord, I'm listening."

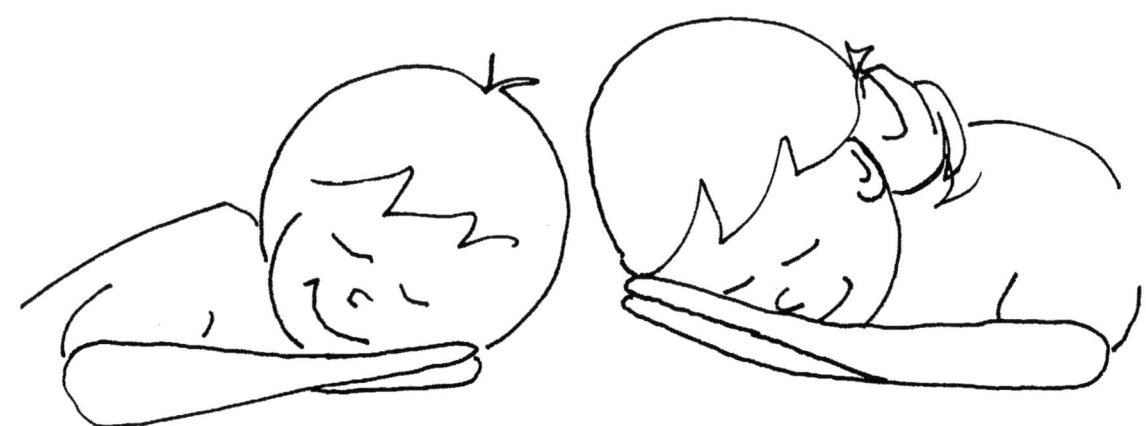

Talk About
1. Who did Samuel think was calling him? Who was it really?
2. Who was taking care of Samuel at night? Does God ever sleep?
3. Who takes care of you at night? Can you talk to God like Samuel did?

Kings and Prophets

Jonathan Eats Honey
1 Samuel 14:24-46

Materials
- a small plastic bag
- honey
- plastic spoons

Prepare Ahead of Time
- Pour honey in the plastic bag.

While You Tell the Story

Lead the children around the room marching, pretending to get more and more tired. Tell how Saul told his army they couldn't have anything to eat all day. Let the children pretend to get more and more hungry. Have the children all sit down together. Tell them about the king's son, Jonathan, who didn't know about that rule. Open up the plastic bag in which you've put honey. Let the children take a look. Tell how Jonathan eats honey and how his eyes brightened when he ate it. Tell how Saul's men thought the rule was a bad one. That's why they are weak and tired. Let the children taste the honey.

Talk About
1. What are some ways you take care of your body? (bathing, brushing teeth, resting, eating healthy food)
2. Why does God want us to take care of our bodies?
3. Was Saul's rule a good one? Why?

Kings and Prophets

David Is Anointed
1 Samuel 16: 1–13

Materials
- old pillowcases
- towels, scarves, belts to use as costumes

While You Tell the Story

Choose one child to be Samuel, one to be David, one to be Jesse, and seven others to be Jesse's sons. Give each actor a costume to wear. Tell the story, gently guiding the children to move to the right places according to your narration.

Samuel thinks that each son is the one he will anoint as he looks at one after another. But tell how God says that none of them is the one. "It's this one...No. It must be this one...No. I'm sure it's this one...No..."

Samuel asks Jesse if he has any other sons. Jesse goes to get David. Then Samuel says that God has told him that this is the one who will be king someday.

Talk About
1. Samuel kept thinking about what these young men looked like. What was God thinking about?
2. Did you ever see people who looked really nice, but didn't act very nice? How can you tell if a person really loves God?
3. God chose David because David loved God. Do you love God? What do you think God has chosen you to do?

Kings and Prophets

David Plays His Harp
1 Samuel 16:14-23; Psalm 145

Materials
- one 8-inch square of heavy cardboard
- plastic drinking straw
- stapler
- large rubber bands
- scissors

Prepare Ahead of Time
• Make a harp by cutting ?-inch slits in two opposite edges of the cardboard as shown. Stretch the rubber bands around the cardboard square, hooking the rubber bands into the slits on each edge. Slide the drinking straw between the rubber bands and the cardboard.
• Make a crown by cutting the yellow paper in half lengthwise. Staple the two pieces together end-to-end, circle them into a ring, and staple to fit a child's head.

While You Tell the Story
Choose one child to be Saul and one to be David. Let Saul wear the crown and have him sit in a chair which will be his "throne." Give David the harp. Tell the story, gently moving the children into place and coaching Saul to smile or frown as needed. Tell how King Saul gets sad and angry. (Frown.) Tell how David would strum on his harp and sing songs for Saul. Tell how this would make Saul feel better. (Smile.) Do this as long as interest lasts.

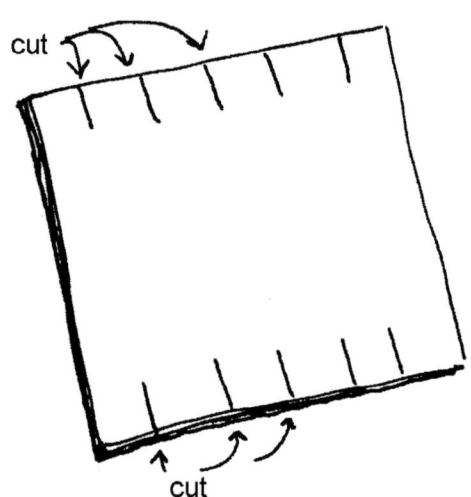
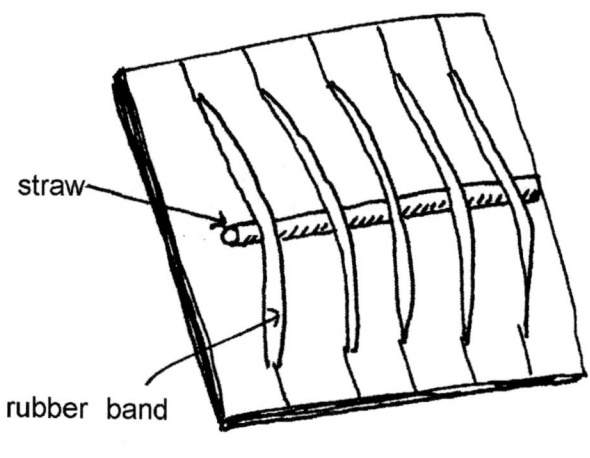

Talk About
1. Why did King Saul want someone to play music for him? How did he feel before he heard the music? How did he feel after he heard it?
2. What did David sing about? What do you like to sing about?
3. David made up his own songs. You can make up your own songs too. What would you say to God if you wrote your own song to him?

Kings and Prophets

David, the Shepherd
1 Samuel 17:15, 34, 35; Psalm 23: 1-4

Materials
- blue bedsheet or tablecloth
- green bedsheet or tablecloth

While You Tell the Story

Spread out the green sheet to make the green pastures. Lay out the blue sheet lengthwise and narrow like a river. Let the children pretend to be sheep. Choose one child to be David, the Shepherd. Let the sheep crawl around and follow the shepherd. Talk about how the sheep need someone to take care of them in spring, summer, fall, and winter. Tell how David cared for his father's sheep and killed wild animals to protect them. Tell what David wrote in Psalm 23. Guide "David" to lead the sheep to the still waters and the green pasture. Tell how David took of sheep, and God takes care of us.

Talk About
1. What does a shepherd do? How did David take care of his sheep?
2. Who took care of David? Who takes care of you?

Kings and Prophets

David and Goliath
1 Samuel 17

Materials
- one 10-foot piece of butcher paper
- markers or crayons
- newspaper
- scissors
- yardstick
- tape
- fabric
- shoestring

Prepare Ahead of Time
- Make a pouch using the pattern on page 164 in the appendix. Cut out a circle of fabric. Weave the shoestring in and out of the holes and tie the ends of the shoestring together.
- Make five stone by crumpling pieces of newspaper.

While You Tell the Story
　　Roll out the butcher paper across the floor. Let the children help measure 9 feet of paper. Draw giant feet at the bottom, a round head at the top, and a belt at the middle. Let the children take turns lying down on the paper. Mark their heights and compare them to Goliath's.

　　Hang the paper on the wall with the feet at floor level. Let the children sit on the floor facing Goliath as you tell the story. Say, "David was little. GOLIATH WAS BIG! David had five stones. GOLIATH HAD A SWORD! But DAVID HAD GOD'S HELP! Goliath had no help."

　　Let the children pick up the newspaper stones to go into the pouch. Let them throw the stones at Goliath.

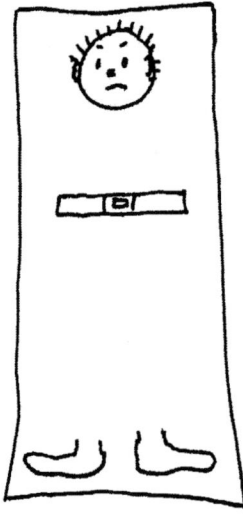

Talk About
1. When David heard Goliath, what did he do?
2. Why was David brave? Who helped David win?
3. Goliath was a big problem. But God helped David. Do you ever have problems? How does God help you?

Kings and Prophets

David and Jonathan
1 Samuel 18:1-4

Materials
- cardboard
- aluminum foil
- robe (made of a large shirt or sweater)
- tunic (cut arm and neck holes in an old pillowcase)
- bow (a plastic clothes hanger held sideways)
- belt (a real belt or strip of cloth)
- scissors
- tape

Prepare Ahead of Time
- Cut out a cardboard sword shape. Cover it with aluminum foil. Use tape as necessary.
- Make a robe, tunic, and bow. Cut the hook off the plastic hanger when making the bow, being sure there are no sharp edges which might hurt the children.

While You Tell the Story

Tell the children that the Bible tells us of two friends. Their names were David and Jonathan. They loved each other very much. They did good things for each other. They shared. Choose one child to be Jonathan and one child to be David.

"One day, Jonathan shared many things with David. Jonathan gave David his robe to wear. And his tunic shirt to wear. And his sword. And his bow, and his belt." As you name each item, Jonathan gives that item to David.

When you've finished telling the story, the child who is David becomes Jonathan, and he chooses another child to be David. Continue to repeat the story, or ask the children to repeat it, choosing a new David each time.

Talk About
1. How did Jonathan show that he was David's friend?
2. What do you share with your friends?
3. How do your friends feel when you share with them?

Kings and Prophets

Abigail Packs Food
1 Samuel 25

Materials
- bread
- juice
- dried beef sticks (for the meat)
- oats
- raisins
- figs
- tray
- small paper cups
- paper towels or hand wipes

Prepare Ahead of Time
- Place each food on a tray.

While You Tell the Story

Ask the children to sit in a circle with you. Place the tray in the middle of the circle. Tell how David and his men needed food and when they asked Abigail's husband, he would not share his food with them. Tell how Abigail decided to prepare and take food to David and his men. Point out the foods that Abigail took to David. Tell how much she took. Let the children taste the foods.

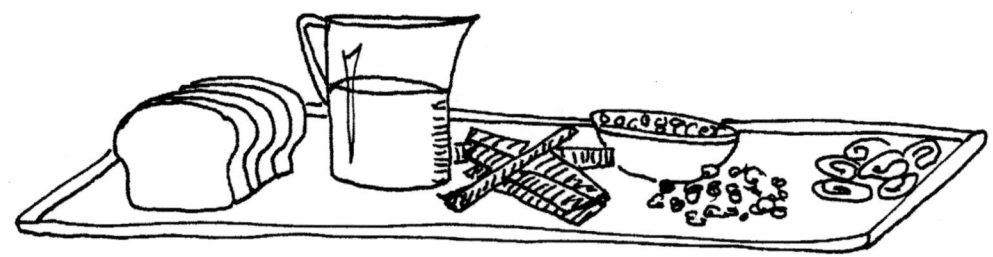

Talk About
1. What do you like to eat when you are hungry?
2. Who was hungry in our story? What did they do?
3. Abigail's husband (Nabal) did not want to share. Was that a good idea or bad?
4. What did Abigail do? Was that a good idea or bad?
5. Does God want us to share? Name some things besides food that we can share?

Kings and Prophets

David and Mephibosheth
2 Samuel 4:4; 9

Materials
- crutch or cane
- bedsheet or tablecloth
- paper plates, cups, napkins
- snack foods, drink

Prepare Ahead of Time
• Make a crutch, if you need to, by cutting down the handle of an old mop and padding the mop head by winding strips of fabric around it.

While You Tell the Story
   Let the children take turns walking with the crutch as you tell the story. Spread the tablecloth on a table or the floor. Set a "king's feast" on it with the snack food, plates, cups, and napkins.
   Tell how David invited Mephibosheth to eat with him at his own table.

Talk About
1. What did David do to be kind to Mephibosheth?
2. Do you know anyone who can't walk (or see or hear)? How can you be kind to them?

Kings and Prophets

Solomon's Dream
1 Kings 3:4-15; 7:1-12; 10:18-21

Materials
- butcher paper
- yellow construction paper
- scissors
- chair
- crayons
- masking tape (push pins or stapler if you have large bulletin board spaces in your room)

Prepare Ahead of Time
- Make the crown by cutting the yellow paper in half lengthwise in a zigzag pattern. Staple the two pieces together, circle them into a ring, and staple to fit a child's head.
- Tack a length of butcher paper along one wall, at the children's height, to make a backdrop.
- Set a chair "throne" in front of everyone.

While You Tell the Story

Choose one child to be Solomon. Let him sit in the throne chair. Ask Solomon to pretend to sleep. Tell about what God and Solomon talked about one night. Then Solomon can wake up.

Tell the children what his palace was like. Draw windows and pillars on the paper on the wall. Choose children to pretend to be the lions on the steps by Solomon's throne.

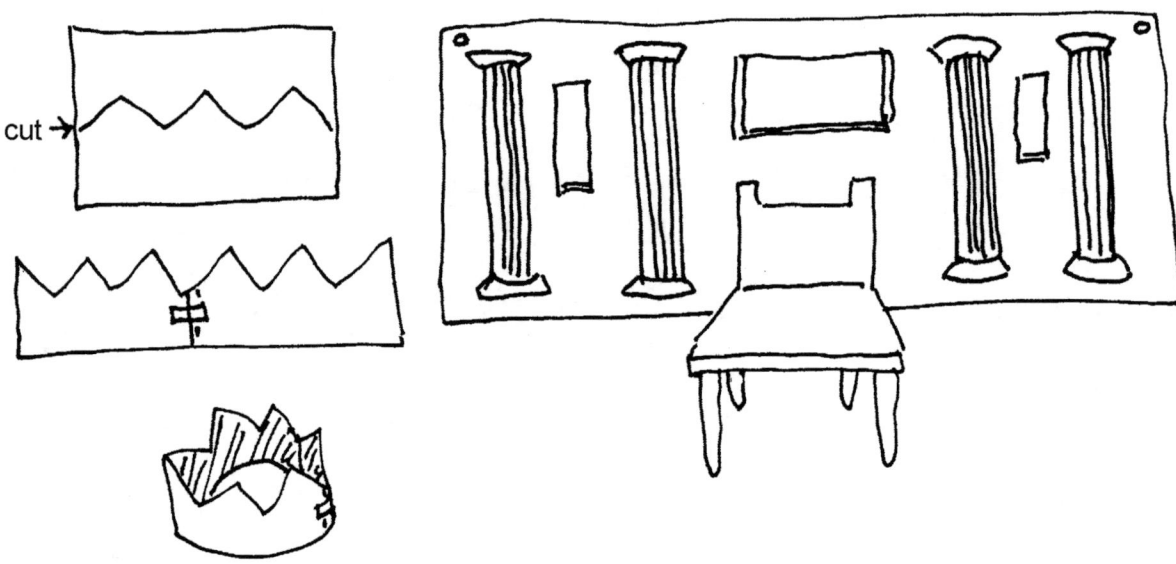

Talk About
1. If God said he'd give you whatever you wanted, what would you ask for?
2. What did Solomon ask God for? How did God feel about that?
3. What did God give Solomon? What are some of the things God has given you?

Kings and Prophets

Solomon Knows About Animals
1 Kings 4:26-34; 10:22-29

Materials
- yellow construction paper
- scissors
- stapler
- chair
- towel
- stuffed animals of different types (optional)

Prepare Ahead of Time
- Make the crown by cutting the yellow paper in half lengthwise in a zigzag pattern. Staple the two pieces together, circle them into a ring, and staple to fit a child's head.
- If you bring stuffed animals, place them around the room.

While You Tell the Story
    Choose one child to be Solomon. Let him sit in the throne chair. Place a towel around his shoulders to make a cloak. Tell how he was interested in animals. (Optional: Have the children look at stuffed animals you've placed around the room.) Make pretend animals by letting the children put their hands above their heads to make animal ears. Ask Solomon to walk around the room, looking at the pretend animals. Then let the children make snakes with one arm. Solomon continues to walk around and look. Have the children make birds by making a fist, then extending thumb and little finger. Solomon walks around and looks. Have the children make fish by putting their hands together, thumbs up. Solomon continues to walk and look. Tell how Solomon had thousands of horses and learned about all types of animals.

Talk About
1. Who made animals?
2. Which animals do you like best?
3. Name some places we see animals. (farm, zoo, our pets at home)
4. What sound does a cow make? A Pig? An Elephant? (Do this as long as time and interest allows.)

Kings and Prophets

The Queen of Sheba
1 Kings 10:1-13

Materials
- two pieces of yellow construction paper
- stapler
- fabric markers or permanent markers
- scissors
- old pillowcase

Prepare Ahead of Time
- Make the crown by cutting the yellow paper in half lengthwise in a zigzag pattern. Staple the two pieces together, circle them into a ring, and staple to fit a child's head.
- Color the pillowcase with markers to make it look like the back of a throne.

While You Tell the Story
   Slip the pillowcase over the back of a chair to make a throne. Choose one child to be King Solomon and one to be the Queen of Sheba. Give each one a crown. Let King Solomon sit on the throne at one side of the room. Everyone else walks around the room, following the queen as she "travels" to see Solomon. Tell about what she saw. She was happy for Solomon and praised God.

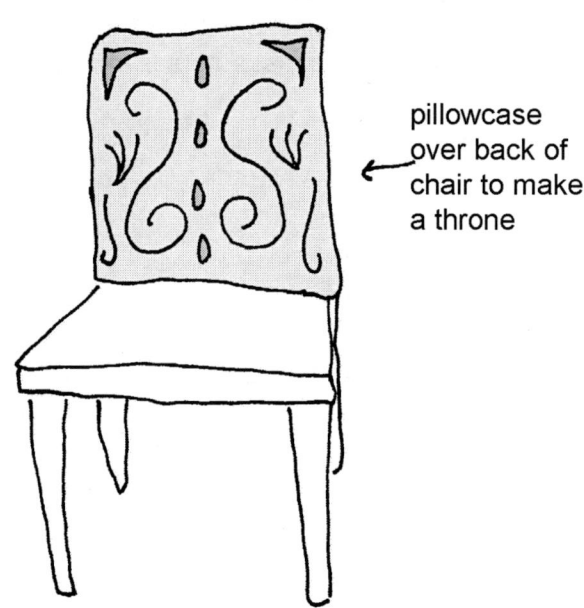

pillowcase over back of chair to make a throne

Talk About
1. Why did the Queen of Sheba visit Solomon? What did she see there?
2. Sometimes people get jealous when they see that other people are rich or smart. They are angry because they don't have that too. How did the Queen of Sheba feel when she saw Solomon's riches and wisdom?
3. The Queen of Sheba praised God because God had given Solomon so much. What has God given you? What can you praise God for?

Kings and Prophets

Ravens Feed Elijah
1 Kings 17:1-6

Materials
- black construction paper
- tape
- reinforcements (for holes of notebook paper)
- beef jerky
- pencil
- string *
- blue bedsheet
- scissors
- water and paper cups
- crackers

Prepare Ahead of Time
• For every bird you want to make, fold a piece of construction paper in half, short ends together. Draw the bird pattern (see page 165 in the appendix) on one side as shown, with its belly on the fold. Cut the bird out, being careful not to cut the fold. Fold the wings down. Place the reinforcement as shown on the pattern page. Tape the bird together at the neck and tail. Thread the string through the reinforcement so the bird can fly. (* Instead of using string, use a drinking straw. Tape the drinking straw to the body of the bird in the center to make a puppet.)
• Slice the beef jerky into bite-sized pieces.

While You Tell the Story
Lay the blue sheet on the floor to make a brook. Seat the children along the sides of the river. Tell the story, flying in the bird(s) when appropriate. When the bird(s) fly in, give each child a cracker and a piece of beef jerky. Let the children drink water. Pretend that it comes from the brook.

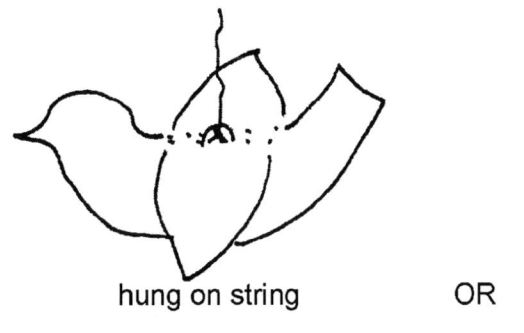

hung on string   OR   held by straw

Talk About
1. Why did Elijah need food? Who was taking care of Elijah? How did God send him food?
2. Does God care when we are hungry and thirsty?
3. How does God take care of you?

Kings and Prophets

A Widow Shares With Elijah
1 Kings 17:8-16

Materials
- flour
- vegetable oil
- two transparent jars
- large bowl, spoon
- skillet, salt, baking powder (optional)

While You Tell the Story

Put 1/4 cup of flour in one jar and 3 teaspoons of oil in the other. Tell the story, letting the children empty the oil and flour from the jars into the bowl and stir them. Point out that the jars are empty. While they are stirring, add another 1/4 cup of flour to one jar and 3 teaspoons of oil to the other. Then ask the children to look. "The jars are not empty. We can make more." Let them add that flour and oil to the bowl and stir them. Continue this way, telling how the widow and her son had food day after day.

If you want to make "bread," for every 1 cup of flour used, add 1/2 teaspoon salt and 1/2 teaspoon baking powder. Cook on a hot skillet until done.

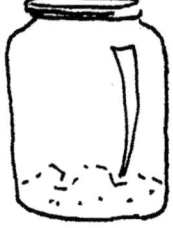  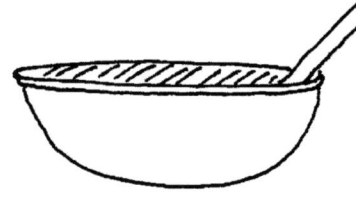

Talk About
1. Who shared in our story? How did God bless the woman?
2. Sharing is part of obeying God. Who can you share with?
3. What are some other things we can share besides food?

Kings and Prophets

Elijah on Mount Carmel
1 Kings 18:18-40

Materials
- brown construction paper
- scissors
- tape
- red, orange, yellow crepe paper

Prepare Ahead of Time
- Cut 5-by-8 inch stones out of the construction paper, one stone for each child.
- Use the crepe paper to make streamers. Cut it into 2-foot lengths.

While You Tell the Story
    Give each child a paper stone. As you tell the story, ask the children to help build an altar by taping the stones to the wall. When the altar is built, the children may sit facing it while you continue the story. When you tell about the fire, tape the streamers to the altar to make the fire.

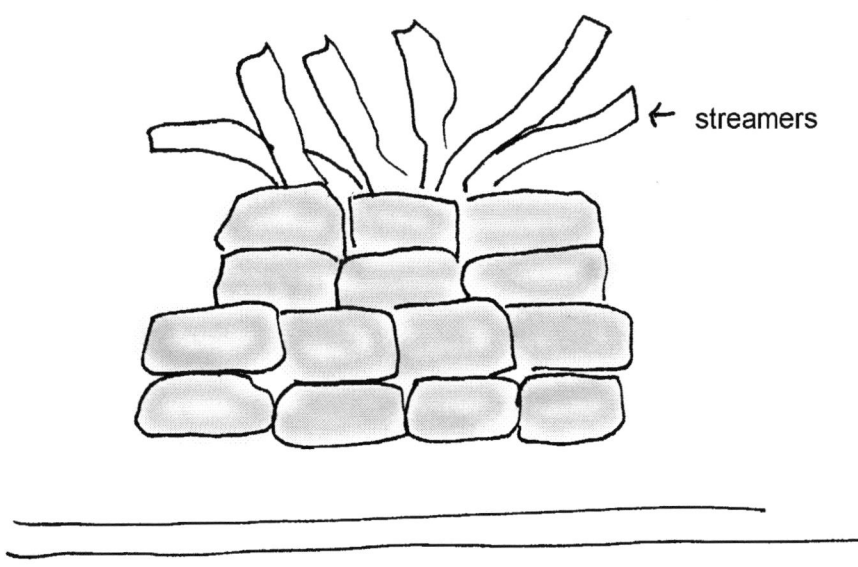
← streamers

Talk About
1. Why did Elijah build an altar?
2. Only God is real. The other people worshiped a fake god, an idol. Who heard the prayer and answered it?
3. Does God hear your prayers? Tell about some wonderful things God has done for you.

61

Kings and Prophets

Elijah and the Cloud
1 Kings 18:41-46

Materials
- three medium-sized paper cups
- two paper fasteners (brads)
- pen or marker
- scissors
- three small bathroom paper cups

Prepare Ahead of Time
- Make a small chariot by cutting a "U" shape out of the top of a medium-sized paper cup, as shown.
- Cut the bottom off of two other medium-sized paper cups and attach them to the chariot with paper fasteners (brads).
- Using small bathroom paper cups, make Elijah, his servant, and Ahab. Draw a face on each cup.

While You Tell the Story
Tell how it hadn't rained in years. Elijah, his servant, and King Ahab were up on a mountain (place them on a chair or table). Tell how Elijah said it was going to rain, and he sent King Ahab back to town in his chariot. Tell the rest of the story, moving the figures around as the story leads.

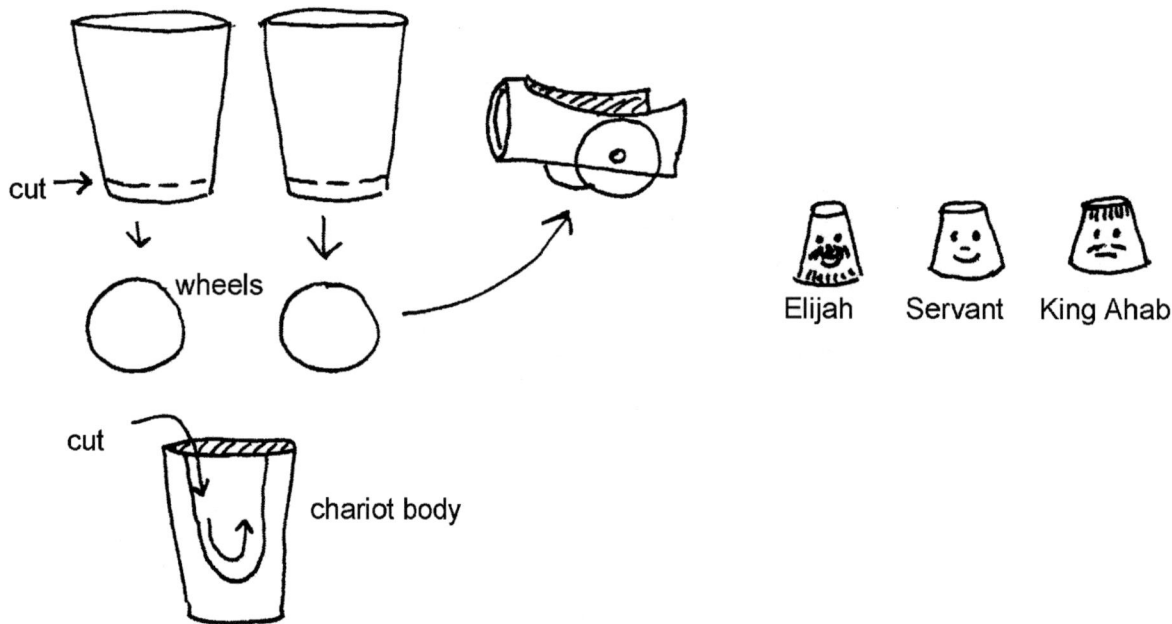

Talk About
1. What did Elijah pray for?
2. What did Elijah tell his servant to do? What did he see?
3. When the rain came, what did the people in the story do?
4. Who took care of Elijah? Who takes care of you?

Kings and Prophets

Elijah in a Cave
1 Kings 19:1-18

Materials
- large sheet
- large piece of stiff cardboard
- orange crepe paper

Prepare Ahead of Time
- Cut five 18-inch lengths of orange crepe paper (streamers).
- Make a cave in your classroom by draping a large sheet over chairs or a table.

While You Tell the Story

Ask the children to get into the cave for story time. Tell them how Elijah was afraid of the mean king and queen because they were angry at him. So he ran away and hid in a cave. He spent the night there. Ask the children to pretend to sleep.

Then tell them what God said to Elijah. Tell how a great wind blew. Wave the cardboard in front of them to make wind blow on them. Pound on the floor to make a rumbling earthquake sound. Wave the streamers back and forth for the fire.

Then speak in a gentle voice while you tell the rest of the story.

Talk About
1. Why was Elijah scared? What did he do?
2. How did God talk to Elijah?
3. What makes you scared? What do you do when you are scared?
4. Who took care of Elijah? Who takes care of you?

Kings and Prophets

Elijah Goes Up to Heaven
1 Kings 19:19-21; 2 Kings 2:1-14

Materials
• two robes (these can be made of pillowcases or towels)
• one blue bedsheet or tablecloth
• red, orange, yellow crepe paper

Prepare Ahead of Time
• Make streamers by cutting the crepe paper into 2-foot lengths.

While You Tell the Story
   Choose one child to be Elijah and one to be Elisha. Let them wear the robes. Tell how Elijah chose Elisha to be his friend and helper. Lay the sheet out on the floor. Help Elijah and Elisha go for a walk as you tell how they walked through the countryside and came to the river. Ask Elijah to take off his robe and hit the water with it. Pull back the sheet so the two men can walk across. Tell how Elisha wanted to be like Elijah (2:9).
   Give each child a red, yellow or orange streamer. Tell about the chariot and horses of fire that came between Elijah and Elisha. Move the two children apart and ask the rest of the children to wave their streamers and run between them to pretend to be the horses of fire.
   Then tell how Elijah dropped his robe and went to Heaven in a whirlwind. The child who is Elijah may sit down. Put the sheet back on the floor. Elisha walks to the sheet and, using Elijah's robe, hits the water with it. Pull the sheet out of the way.
   You might want to repeat the story with two other children acting as Elijah and Elisha.

Talk About
1. Elijah and Elisha were good friends. Who are your good friends?
2. Why do you think Elisha wanted to be like Elijah? Who do you want to be like?

Kings and Prophets

A Widow's Oil Jars
2 Kings 4:1-7

Materials
- lots of plastic jars or paper cups
- pitcher

Prepare Ahead of Time
- Before you tell the story, set the jars or cups in different places all around the room.

While You Tell the Story

Tell the children about the woman's problem and what Elisha told her to do. Ask the children to go get the jars from around the room. But before they pick up a jar, they must knock on something like they're knocking on a neighbor's door. When they return to you with all of the jars, pretend to pour oil from your pitcher into two cups. Then say, "That's all the oil I have." Look in the pitcher and exclaim, "No! There's more!" Continue this until all of the cups or jars are "full."

Tell about the woman selling the oil and paying back the money her husband owed.

Talk About
1. How did Elisha help the woman?
2. How did the woman's boys help her?
3. How do you help your family?

Kings and Prophets

Elisha's Room on the Roof
2 Kings 4:8-17

Materials
- none

While You Tell the Story

When you tell about the room the woman made for Elisha, choose children to be the furniture in the room. They mime whatever piece of furniture you have chosen them to be. For example, the "table" gets down on all fours. The "chair" sits cross-legged with arms to be chair arms. The "bed" sits on the floor with legs straight out. The "lamp" stands straight. When you "turn" the lamp's ear, the eyes close, indicating the light is off. When you turn the ear again, the eyes open, indicating the light is on. Choose a child to be Elisha, and show him around the room.

Another idea: Use small toy figures to represent the lady, her husband, and Elisha. Turn a box upside down to make their house. Draw or cut a door and windows in it. Tell the first part of the story. To build Elisha's room, turn a smaller box over and put it on top of the first box. The children can make sawing and hammering motions with their hands.

Talk About
1. How was the woman kind to Elisha?
2. How did Elisha feel about it? How do you think the woman felt?
3. How can you be kind to your friends? How can you be kind to your family? Being kind is one way to obey God.

Kings and Prophets

Elisha and the Stew
2 Kings 4:38-41

Materials
- big cooking pot and spoon
- blocks
- flashlight
- green or orange construction paper

Prepare Ahead of Time
- Cut out several circles from the construction paper. These circles will represent the fruit and vegetables in the story.

While You Tell the Story

Have the children help you build a "campfire" by stacking blocks around a flashlight. Turn on the flashlight and set the cooking pot on the blocks. Let the children stir. Tell how Elisha's friends are cooking stew. Pretend to put vegetables in. Tell how one man puts in a plant he found. Then pretend to be the man who put in the gourds or fruit. Toss in some of the construction paper circles. Tell how the stew is poisoned, but Elisha makes it good again.

Talk About
1. Who made plants? Can you name some plants?
2. God made some plants to eat and some just to look at. We never eat plants we find. Who should we ask if a plant is for eating?
3. Who was cooking in our story? What happened?

> Kings and Prophets

Naaman
2 Kings 5:1-19

Materials
- baby powder
- blue bedsheet

Prepare Ahead of Time
- Practice the "Naaman Song" below so you are familiar with it.

While You Tell the Story

Spread a blue sheet on the floor to make the Jordan River. Sprinkle baby powder on the children's arms so they can pretend to be Naaman with leprosy. Tell about Naaman's skin sickness and how the little girl told him to go see Elisha, a man of God. Let the children do the actions in a circle with you as you lead them in the "Naaman Song."

Naaman Song (Tune: "The Farmer in the Dell")

Verse 1
Naaman was sick,   (hold out arms)
Naaman was sick.
His skin turned white! Oh, what a sight!
For Naaman was sick.

Verse 2
He went to see Elisha,   (march around in a
He went to see Elisha.   circle)
He heard that he could make him well.
He went to see Elisha.

Verse 3
Elisha said, "Go wash,"   (dip up and down)
Elisha said, "Go wash."
Dip in the river seven times.
Elisha said, "Go wash"

Verse 4
"That's silly!" Naaman said,   (hands on hips
"That's silly!" Naaman said.   shake head)
"Whoever heard of such a thing?"
"That's silly!" Naaman said.

Verse 5
"Just do it anyway,"   (shake forefinger)
"Just do it anyway."
His helpers helped him to decide.
"Just do it anyway."

Verse 6
So Naaman obeyed.   (dip up and down)
So Naaman obeyed.
He washed in the river seven times.
So Naaman obeyed.

Verse 7
Then Naaman was well,   (arms stretched out
Then Naaman was well.   and up)
He said, "I now believe in God."
Then Naaman was well.

Talk About
1. At first, Naaman didn't believe in God. Why did he go to see Elisha?
2. Do you ever get sick? How do you get well?
3. Naaman didn't want to obey at first. What happened when he obeyed? Why is it important to obey God?

Kings and Prophets

Elisha's Servant Sees God's Army
2 Kings 6:15-19

Materials
- butcher paper
- tape
- glue
- copies of the horses and chariots pattern from page 166 in the appendix
- blue construction paper

Prepare Ahead of Time
- Stretch the butcher paper across the wall and secure it with tape or thumbtacks.
- Make several copies of the horses and chariots of God (fire) and of the enemies from the pattern in the appendix. Glue the horses and chariots of fire along the top section of the butcher paper.
- Glue the enemies along the bottom section of the butcher paper.
- Tape blue construction paper over the horses and chariots of fire, so the blue paper looks like the sky.

While You Tell the Story
   Tell how Elisha's servant is afraid because he sees the enemies. Tell how Elisha prayed to God. When God reveals his army, take the blue paper off the horses and chariots of fire. Tell how Elisha's servant saw God's army.

Talk About
1. Name some places where God is with us.
2. Where is God when you sleep? God is everywhere.
3. Who was God with in our story? What happened?

Kings and Prophets

King Hezekiah Gets Well
2 Kings 20:1-11; Isaiah 38:1-20

Materials
- two small story figures (See appendix A for suggestions.)
- flashlight
- blocks

Prepare Ahead of Time
- Ask the children to help you build a stairway out of blocks for the small story figures.

While You Tell the Story

Move the story figures as you tell how Hezekiah got sick. You can use a block to be his bed. Show Isaiah coming to see him. When you get to the part about the shadow, place a figure on the block stairs and shine a flashlight on the stairs. Make a shadow that moves forward and one that moves backward. Tell about Hezekiah's choice and show the shadow movement. Tell about the song Hezekiah wrote to thank God.

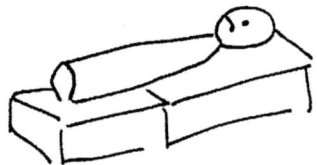

Talk About
1. Hezekiah wanted to get well. What did he do?
2. What do you do when you get sick? Who can make you well?
3. Hezekiah wrote a thank-you song to God. What can you thank God for?
4. What are some other ways we can thank God?

Kings and Prophets

King Josiah Finds God's Word
2 Kings 22:1–23:3

Materials
- one piece of yellow construction paper
- scissors
- stapler
- small Bible
- several shoe boxes, other boxes with lids to represent bricks
- a variety of small items: crumpled paper, a rock, a candy wrapper

Prepare Ahead of Time
- Make a crown by cutting the construction paper lengthwise in a zigzag pattern. Place the ends of the paper together and staple it to fit a child's head.
- Put the Bible in one box, and put each of the other items in a box.
- Before telling the story, randomly set the boxes on the floor.

While You Tell the Story
　　Choose one child to be King Josiah. Tell the story. Ask the children to pretend with you to be helpers in the worship house. Pretend to dust and sweep. Use the boxes to build up the wall. Let the children find the items in the boxes.
　　When you find the Bible, take it to the king. Read a few of the commandments: obey your father and mother, use God's name respectfully, do not steal, and so on. Guide the king and the group to decide to obey the rules.
　　You may reenact this using someone else as the king, and letting a child hide the Bible for others to find again.

Talk About
1. What did the workers find? What did the king think when he read it?
2. What did the people do?
3. Are these rules God wants us to obey too? Why does God give us rules?

Kings and Prophets

Jehoshaphat's Army
2 Chronicles 20:1-30

Materials
• rhythm instruments

While You Tell the Story

Tell the story, asking the children to kneel and pray when you tell how all the people prayed. After you tell them what God said (verses 15-17), ask the children to clap and cheer and say, "Praise God."

Then give the children rhythm instruments. March around the room playing the instruments as you tell about the singers and musicians leading the army out. Tell about what happened to the enemies.

Optional: As the children march around the room, have them sing the following song to the tune of "Mary Had a Little Lamb."

Everybody thank the Lord, thank the Lord, thank the Lord.
Everybody thank the Lord, his love lasts forever.

Talk About
1. How did Jehoshaphat feel when he found out that the enemy was coming? What did he do?
2. What makes you scared or worried? What do you do?
3. How did God help Jehoshaphat? How does God help you?

Kings and Prophets

Taking Care of the Worship House
1 Chronicles 9:22-34

Materials
• bring several types of kitchen tools, dishes, foods, and rhythm instruments.
• one piece of yellow construction paper
• scissors
• stapler

Prepare Ahead of Time
• Make a crown by cutting the construction paper lengthwise in a zigzag pattern. Place the ends of the paper together and staple it to fit a child's head.
• Place the tools and dishes in one area of the room, food in another area, and rhythm instruments in another area.

While You Tell the Story
Choose one child to be King David. Put the paper crown on his head. Tell how David chose different men to take care of the worship house. Tell how the men were gatekeepers and they did a good job. As you tell about the people in charge, ask the king to choose children to go to those areas of the room to take care of the worship house.

Talk About
1. Does your room where you live ever get messy?
2. How do you take care of your room? Your other possessions (toys, clothes)?
3. Does God wants us to take care of our rooms and possessions? Why?
4. How did the people in our story take care of the worship house?

Kings and Prophets

Ezra Reads God's Words
Nehemiah 8:1-12

Materials
- two paper plates
- stapler
- pen or marker

Prepare Ahead of Time
- Make a puppet by stapling two paper plates together. Leave an opening for your hand to fit inside. Draw a smiling face on one side and a frowning face on the other.

While You Tell the Story
    Tell how Ezra read God's Word to the people from the time the sun came up until lunchtime. Show the puppet how the people reacted when God's Word was read. Tell how the people were sad because they hadn't heard God's Words in a long time. Tell how Ezra told the people to cheer up and celebrate.

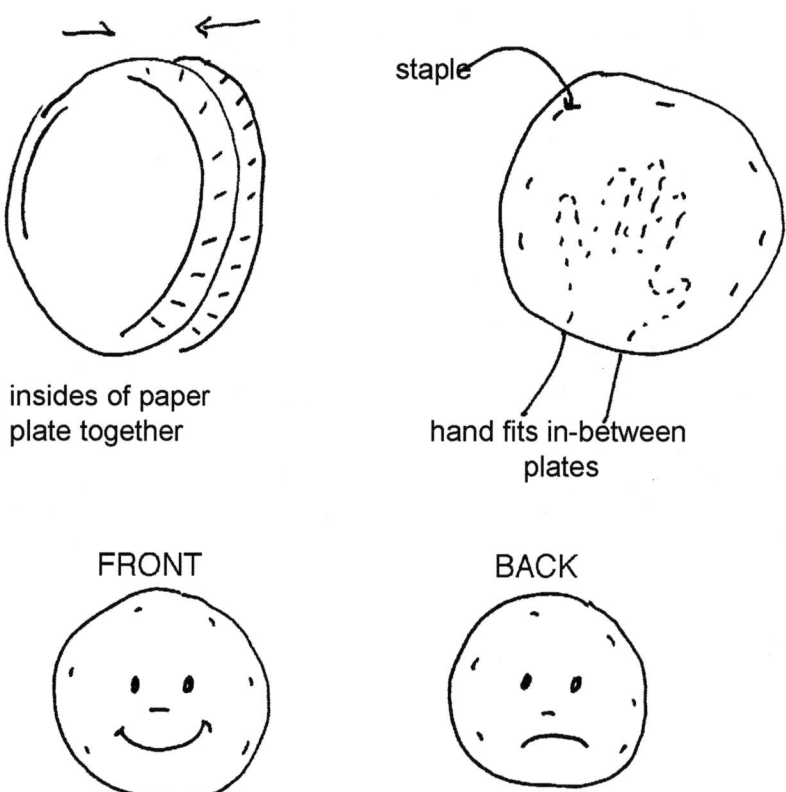

Talk About
1. What does the Bible tell us?
2. When do you hear Bible stories? Which story is your favorite?
3. Who loved the Bible in our story?

Kings and Prophets

Recab's Family
Jeremiah 35

Materials
- pitcher and clear plastic picnic cups
- purple drink (grape juice or Kool-Aid)
- table and chairs or tablecloth

Prepare Ahead of Time
- Prepare the drink.

While You Tell the Story
    Seat everyone around the table or cloth on the floor. Place a pitcher of purple drink in the middle of the table. Give each child a clear plastic picnic cup. Tell the story, pretending the children are Recab's family. Tell how Jeremiah set out wine for Recab's family to drink. Tell how they will not drink wine because Recab said not to. Tell how God said his people should obey Him like Recab's family obeyed Recab.

Talk About
1. What does it mean to obey? Who does God want us to obey?
2. What rules do you obey at home?
3. Did the people in the story obey or disobey? What happened?

Kings and Prophets

Daniel Refuses the King's Food
Daniel 1

Materials
- one paper plate for each child
- several magazine pictures of junk food
- one picture of good food for each child

Prepare Ahead of Time
- Cut out the pictures of junk food and good food.

While You Tell the Story

Tell about Daniel and his friends at the king's palace. Tell them about the king's table. Divide the children into two groups. Practice with one group saying, "Mmm, mmmm. Yes, I want it." Practice with the other group saying, "No way. God says, 'No.'"

Talk about how Daniel and his friends had to choose. They might have really wanted to eat some of the king's food. It probably looked and smelled very good. So part of Daniel's mind might have been saying, "Mmm, mmmm. Yes, I want it." But he controlled himself. He knew he shouldn't eat it.

Show pictures of the junk food, one at a time. After each picture, let group 1 say their response; then group 2. Now give each child a plate and let the children choose pictures of good food to put on their plates. Talk about what happened when Daniel and his friends ate the good food.

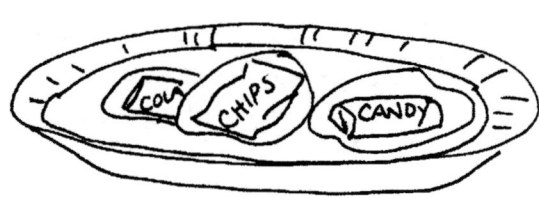 

Talk About
1. Self-control is making yourself do what you know you should do. How did Daniel show self-control?
2. Do you choose what to eat sometimes? How do you show self-control?
3. Eating good food helps us stay healthy. What are some other things that help us stay healthy?

Kings and Prophets

Daniel Thanks God
Daniel 2

Materials
- large piece of paper
- marker or pen for teacher
- crayons

Prepare Ahead of Time
- Draw a big, simple statue on a large piece of paper.

While You Tell the Story

Ask the children to cross their arms as you tell about the king. They should look sad and scared when you tell about the wise men. Tell how the king had a bad dream that kept him awake. The king asked all the wise men to tell him what his dream was about. Tell how the king wanted to kill all the wise men unless they could tell him about his dream. Ask the children to fold their hands to pray. Tell how Daniel prayed and asked God to tell him what the king's dream was about. When God told Daniel what the dream was about, Daniel thanked God and then went to tell the king. Ask the children to clap and say, "Thank-you, God!"

Let the children color in the parts of the statue as you tell them about the dream:

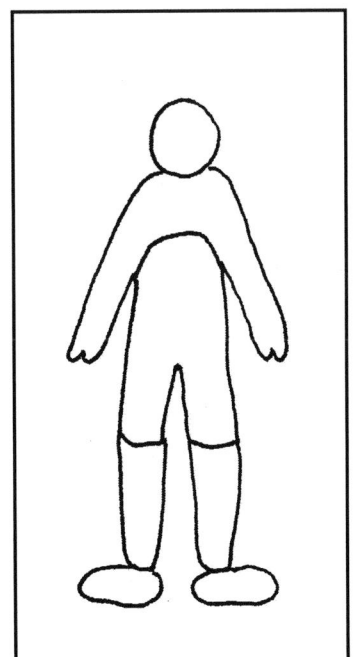

1. gold head

2. silver chest and arms

3. brown torso and thighs

4. gray lower legs

5. gray and tan feet

Talk about the king's dream and the meaning. (Kings don't last forever–like the statue that gets knocked over. But Jesus is our king. He lasts forever–like the rock that doesn't move.)

Talk About
1. What was the king's dream in the story? What did it mean?
2. When God told Daniel about the dream, what did Daniel do?
3. What can you thank God for?

Kings and Prophets

The Fiery Furnace
Daniel 3

Materials
- tall man doll (like a Ken doll)
- small men figures, at least five: the king, three Israelite friends, the fourth person in the furnace (see appendix A for suggestions)
- shoe box
- yellow and orange tissue paper for flames in the shoe box furnace
- aluminum foil

Prepare Ahead of Time
- Wrap aluminum foil around the tall doll to make an idol.
- Put the tissue paper inside the shoe box to look like flames.

While You Tell the Story
Tell the story, using the tall doll as the idol. Use the other figures to walk through the rest of the story.

Another idea: Bring a big box and set it up with the opening at the top. Let the children color it to look like a fire is all around it. Choose three children to be Daniel's friends. Tell the story. When the three are thrown into the fire, let the three get into the box and walk around. You can squeeze cellophane in your hand to make a fire crackling sound. Ask the children to count them aloud with you. Place a fourth child in the box. Count them again.

Talk About
1. Do you think it was easy for Shadrach, Meshach, and Abednego to disobey the king's orders?
   Why did they disobey? Who were they obeying?
2. What did everyone else do? Can you think of a time when it would be hard for you to do right?
3. Is it easy to choose to do right when everyone else is doing wrong?
4. Who took care of Shadrach, Meshach, and Abednego? Who takes care of you?

Kings and Prophets

Writing on the Wall
Daniel 5

Materials
- one 4-foot length of butcher paper
- paper cups, paper plates, napkins
- grapes, apple slices, bananas
- black crayon
- aluminum foil
- tablecloth

Prepare Ahead of Time
- Tape the butcher paper onto the wall.
- Wrap the paper cups with foil to make goblets.

While You Tell the Story

Put the tablecloth on the table or floor. Set out the plates, napkins, and fruit. Let the children eat as you tell the story. Write the words "mene, mene, tekel, parsin" on the butcher paper when you get to that part of the story. Demonstrate how the king's knees knocked together and he had to sit down. Tell the rest of the story.

Talk About
1. King Belshazzar was worshiping idols. What's an idol?
2. God wants us to worship only him. How do we worship God?
3. How did Daniel know what the handwriting said?

> Kings and Prophets

Daniel and the Lions
Daniel 6

Materials
- puppet shadow theater (see appendix B for instructions)
- black construction paper
- scissors
- drinking straws
- tape
- small lamp
- clay or play dough

Prepare Ahead of Time
- Cut from the black construction paper the figures shown in the pattern on page 167. Attach the figures to drinking straws using tape.
- Set up the puppet shadow theater with the lamp shining behind it.

While You Tell the Story
　　Darken the room. Tell the story by moving the figures behind the tissue paper openings, so that the children see shadows of the story figures. Stand up the figures of the lions by sticking the straws into clay or play dough.

Another idea: Choose one child to be Daniel and one to be the angel. For angel wings, cut down one side of a paper grocery sack. Cut the bottom off. Lay the paper flat and fold it accordion-style horizontally. Staple the folded layers together in the center. Let the sides fan out. Pin it to the angel's back. Tell the story, moving Daniel and the angel around as the story leads. Let the other children roar and act like lions as they sit in a circle.

> **Talk About**
> 1. How did the king feel about Daniel? Why?
> 2. Had Daniel done anything wrong? Why was he thrown into the lion's den? What happened there?
> 3. Who took care of Daniel? Who takes care of you?

Kings and Prophets

Jonah
Jonah 1–3

Materials
- toy boat or ship (Make this out of a box if you need to.)
- small figure of a man (See appendix A for suggestions.)
- fish sock puppet

Prepare Ahead of Time
- Make the fish sock puppet as shown with felt fins and tail sewn on and button eyes.

While You Tell the Story
   Tell the story, making the boat sway back and forth, up and down, higher and higher during the storm. Throw the Jonah figure overboard. Use the fish to come and swallow Jonah, and later spit him on the land.

Another idea: Bring a big box (a box for a large kitchen appliance). Turn it so that the opening is on one side. Draw a big fish on the side of the box and let the children color it with crayons and markers. Tell the story of Jonah, asking the children to sway back and forth when the storm comes. Flash the lights off and on to make lightning. Ask the children to pat the floor to make rumbling wave sounds. Let the children take turns going into the box and jumping out when Jonah is tossed out onto the land.

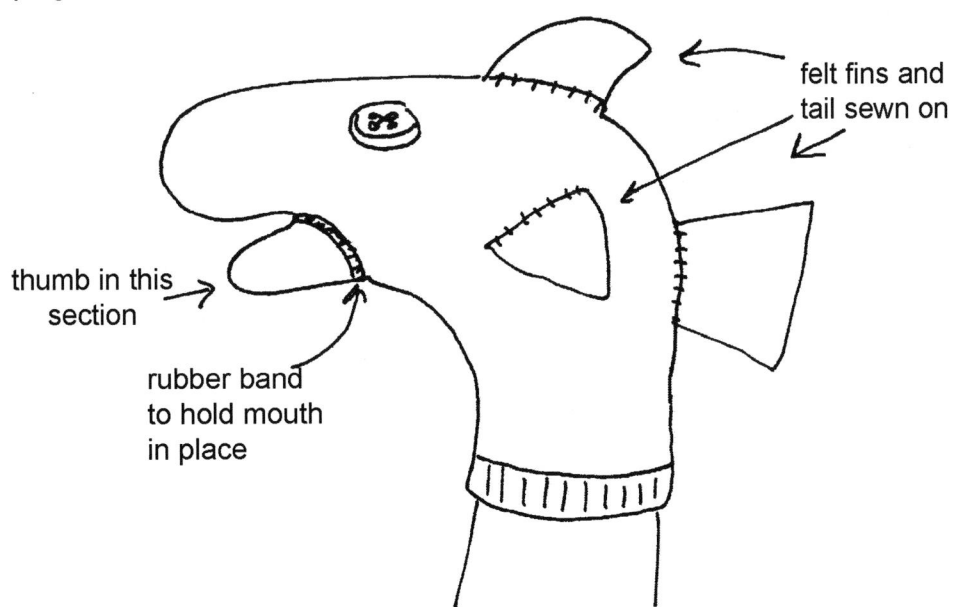

Talk About
1. Jonah tried to run away from God. Could he hide from God?
2. Who was taking care of Jonah? God was with him everywhere. Is God with you everywhere?
3. What did God want Jonah to do? Did Jonah obey? Who do you obey?

Jesus' Life, Death, and Resurrection

Zechariah Cannot Speak
Luke 1:5-25, 57-66

Materials
- handkerchief or square of white or yellow cloth
- string or ribbon
- small paper plate
- craft stick
- large cotton ball
- scissors
- markers or crayons
- tape or glue

Prepare Ahead of Time
• Make the angel by placing the cotton ball in the center of the handkerchief. Bring the rest of the handkerchief up around the cotton ball and tie it there with string or ribbon, leaving enough room to place your index finger into the cotton, as shown.
• Make a Zechariah puppet by drawing a talking face on one side of the plate and a silent face on the other. Tape or glue a craft stick to the plate so you can hold it up.

While You Tell the Story
   Ask the children to be the people outside the temple waiting for Zechariah to come out. They fold their hands, ready to pray and worship.
   Show the talking side of the Zechariah puppet and tell about how he was in the temple preparing for the worship when an angel come.
   With the angel puppet on your other hand, tell about the angel's message, Zechariah's reaction, and the sign that the angel gave: that Zechariah would not be able to speak until John was born.
   Tell the rest of the story, turning the Zechariah puppet back around when the baby is named.

Talk About
1. What was the promise God gave to Zechariah? Did Zechariah believe it? Did the promise come true?
2. What kinds of promises does God give to you and me? Can we believe God? Does he keep his promises? We can trust God.

Jesus' Life, Death, and Resurrection

Gabriel Appears to Mary
Luke 1:26-38

Materials
- brown, paper grocery sack*
- safety pin
- scissors
- old pillowcase

Prepare Ahead of Time
• Cut down the side of a brown, paper grocery sack, and cut off the bottom of the bag. Open out the remaining sack. Fold it accordion-style, lengthwise.
• Cut a neck hole and armholes out of the closed end of an old pillowcase. Cut from the open end through the middle of one side up to the neck hole. This makes a long vest.
• Place a safety pin the middle of the folded paper and pin to the center of the back of the vest. Fan the paper out to make wings.

While You Tell the Story
Choose one child to wear the angel vest and be Gabriel. Tell the children to pretend the are Mary. As you tell the story, ask them to show expressions on their faces reflecting how Mary might have felt: fear, surprise, wonder, joy.
Tell how God sent the angel Gabriel to see Mary. Tell how Gabriel tells Mary she will have a baby—God's Son. Tell how Mary wondered about it, but says she will do what God wants.
* Option: Instead of a grocery sack, use tissue paper or "metallic" gift wrap.

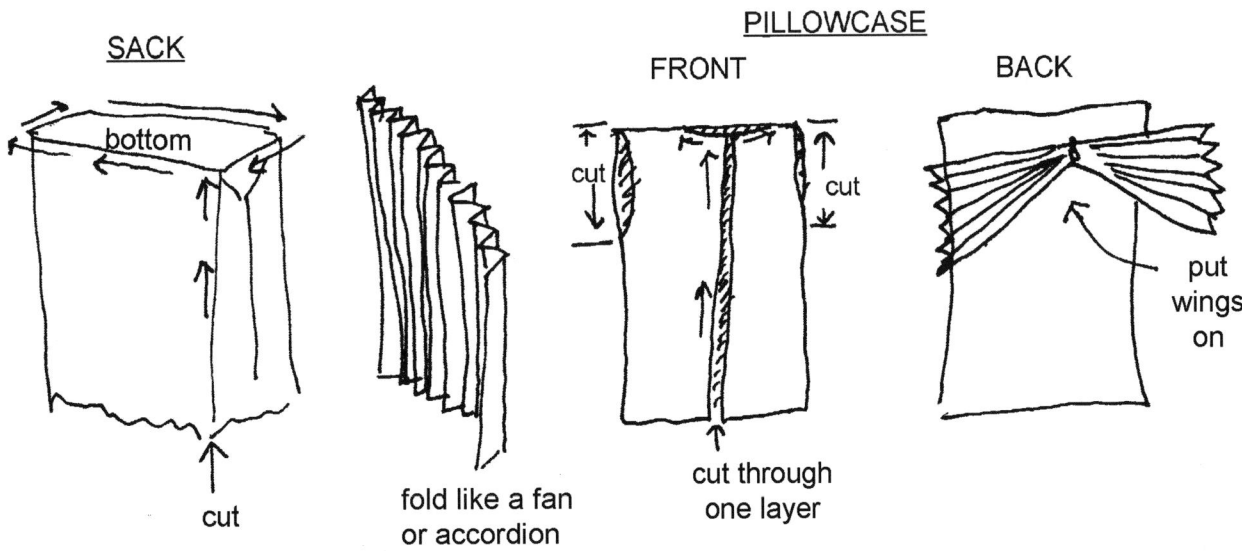

Talk About
1. Who sent the angel in our story? Why did the angel come?
2. Who sent baby Jesus? Who was baby Jesus?

> Jesus' Life, Death, and Resurrection

Mary Praises God
Luke 1:26-56

Materials
- none

While You Tell the Story

Tell how Mary knew she was going to have a special baby, God's Son. Let the children pretend to pack their bags. Walk around the room pretending to go on a journey to see Elizabeth. Let the children suggest other ways of moving: jumping, running, skipping, and so on. When you get to Elizabeth's house, sit down and rest. Read or tell what Mary said to praise God.

Talk About
1. How did Mary know she was going to have a special baby?
2. Where did Mary go? Why?
3. Mary praised God. How did she praise God?
4. What are some ways we can praise God?

> Jesus' Life, Death, and Resurrection

Jesus Is Born
Luke 2:1-7

Materials
- piece of paper
- nativity pattern (page 168 in the appendix)
- scissors

Prepare Ahead of Time
- Copy the pattern onto a piece of paper. Practice cutting out the picture. Place the dotted line on the fold of the paper and cut on the solid line.

While You Tell the Story

Set the chairs around the room with the chair backs facing the center of the room. The children can kneel behind the chairs or sit backwards in them, looking into the center of the room. Choose one child to be Joseph and one to be Mary. If you can find someone who likes to give children rides on his back, invite him to be the donkey that Mary rides.

Tell Joseph to lead Mary and the donkey around the room to each chair (inn). When Joseph knocks on the door (the chair), the child behind the chair says, "No room!" When Joseph has been to all of the inns, ask, "Where can they stay?" Let the children answer. Talk about what a stable is. Then fold and cut the paper with the copied nativity pattern. As you cut, tell how baby Jesus was born that night in the stable.

> **Talk About**
> 1. Why couldn't Mary and Joseph find a place to stay?
> 2. What's a stable? What's a manger? If you had to sleep in a stable, where would you sleep?
> 3. Who was baby Jesus? Why did God send his Son?

> Jesus' Life, Death, and Resurrection

Angels Appear to the Shepherds
Luke 2:8-20

Materials
- handkerchiefs or squares of cloth (one per child)
- string or ribbon
- large cotton balls
- scissors

Prepare Ahead of Time
- Make angels out of the handkerchiefs, cotton balls, and string as shown.

While You Tell the Story
   Give each child an angel to put on his hand as shown. Tell the story of the shepherds and their sheep on the hillside. When you get to the part where the angels appear, let all of the children lift up their angels. Practice saying, "Glory to God in the highest. Peace on earth." Sing together "Hark the Herald Angels Sing."

Another idea: Use large cotton balls to represent sheep. For eyes, make two dots with a permanent marker; add small felt ears. Use toy figures, clothespin figures, or shepherd figures from a nativity scene. Make the puppet angels (above) and let the children fly them through the air as you tell the story.

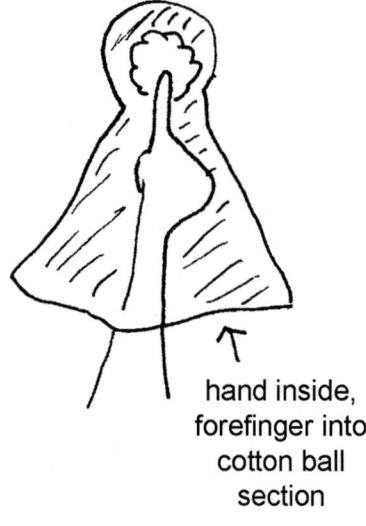

hand inside, forefinger into cotton ball section

> **Talk About**
> 1. What were the shepherds doing? How did they feel when they saw the angels?
> 2. Why did the angels come? What did they say?
> 3. Why did God send baby Jesus?

Jesus' Life, Death, and Resurrection

The Wise Men
Matthew 2:1-12

Materials
- butcher paper
- wise men
- small paper bathroom cup
- crayons
- shoebox
- play dough
- paper star
- scissors

Prepare Ahead of Time
- Use nativity figures for wise men, or make clothespin figures and pretzel camels. (See appendix A for suggestions.)
- Cut a star out of paper and put it on the wall above the house.
- Roll out butcher paper across the floor and part way up a wall as shown. Draw a road that sometimes goes straight and sometimes curves left or right all the way down the paper. At one end, place a shoebox on its side so the opening faces out. This is the house.
- Cut out the bottom of a small paper bathroom cup to make the baby's bed. Two small balls of play dough can be the baby's head and body.

While You Tell the Story
   Let the children move the figures down the road to the house. Tell how a special star showed in the sky and the wise men followed the star to find a baby king. Tell how the wise men find baby Jesus and gave him gifts.

Talk About
1. How did the wise men know where to go? Why did they go there?
2. What did the wise men do when they found the child Jesus?
3. Who is Jesus? Why did God send Jesus?

Jesus' Life, Death, and Resurrection

Jesus as a Boy in the Temple
Luke 2:41-52

Materials
- two pieces of plain white paper
- tape
- scissors

While You Tell the Story

As you tell the story, tape the two pieces of plain white paper together at the narrow end. Fold them together and cut a diagonal line, as shown. Then fold it accordion-style and cut out the section indicated in the illustration. When you talk about Mary and Joseph finding Jesus in the temple, open the paper and show the temple you've cut out.

Another idea: Drape a sheet over two chairs to make the worship house. The children pretend with you to be Mary and Joseph. Walk around the room, on the way home. Start asking, "Where is Jesus?" Walk back to Jerusalem, and hunt here and there as if looking for Jesus. At last, find him in the worship house. Tell the children that Jesus was listening to the teachers there.

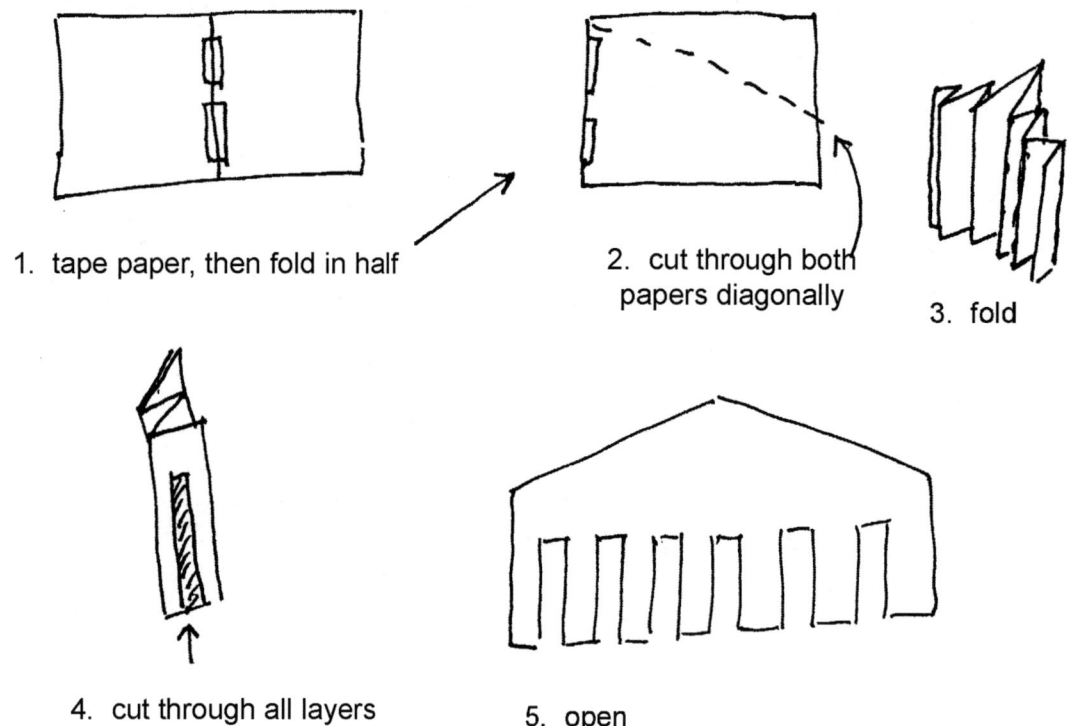

1. tape paper, then fold in half
2. cut through both papers diagonally
3. fold
4. cut through all layers
5. open

Talk About
1. What was Jesus doing in the temple?
2. When Mary and Joseph found Jesus, what did Jesus do? Did he obey them?

Jesus' Life, Death, and Resurrection

Jesus Grew

Luke 2:52; Matthew 13:53-58

Materials
- none

While You Tell the Story

Tell or read what the people said about Jesus in Matthew 13:53-58. Teach the children this action verse:

Jesus was a little child just like you	(squat down).
But he didn't stay little, he grew and grew	(rise slowly).
And that is just what you will do	(stretch arms up).

Point out that Jesus had brothers and sisters. Jesus' father on earth was a carpenter. He built things. Tell how Jesus grew up obeying his mother and Joseph.

Talk About
1. Do you have brothers and sisters? What do you do with them?
2. What job does your dad and/or mom have?
3. Are you growing bigger or smaller? How have you changed since you were a baby?
4. Who makes us grow? Who was growing in our story?

Jesus' Life, Death, and Resurrection

John the Baptist
Matthew 3:1-6

Materials
• grasshopper in a jar or a picture of a grasshopper
• honey

Prepare Ahead of Time
• If you can catch a grasshopper, bring it in a jar. If not, bring a picture of a grasshopper. (You may copy the picture on this page or look for a grasshopper picture in a book or encyclopedia.)

While You Tell the Story
    Ask the children to look at the grasshopper or the picture of the grasshopper. Tell about John living in the desert, dressing in clothes made of camel's hair and eating grasshoppers and wild honey. Let the children taste the honey. Tell them what John did to tell people Jesus was coming.

Talk About
1. What did John tell people? Why?
2. What did John eat? What do you like to eat?
3. Who gives us our food?

Jesus' Life, Death, and Resurrection

Jesus Is Tempted
Matthew 4:1-11

Materials
- loaf of bread
- chair

While You Tell the Story

Set out a loaf of bread as you tell about the first temptation. Ask a small child to stand on a chair as you tell about the temptation to jump off of the temple. Hold a child up on a classroom table, or if a male volunteer is available, let him lift a child onto his shoulders as you tell about Jesus surveying the earth and being tempted to worship the devil.

Talk About
1. Can we encourage each other to do right? How?
2. If someone is encouraging us to do wrong, what should we do?
3. Tell of a time when someone you know encouraged another person to do right. What happened?

Jesus' Life, Death, and Resurrection

Jesus Chooses Twelve Friends
Matthew 4:18-22; 9;9; 10:2-4;
John 1:43-49

Materials
- none

While You Tell the Story
    Ask the children to pretend to rock in a boat. Choose four to follow you. Tell how Jesus chose Peter, Andrew, James and John at the lake.
    Ask the children to pretend to ride a donkey down the road. Choose one from the "tax booth." Ask the children to hold arms up like trees. Choose one from under the fig tree. Tell how Jesus chose Matthew at work and Nathanael who was under a fig tree.
    Choose six more. Tell who Jesus chose Philip, Thomas, another James, Thaddaeus, Simon, and Judas.
    Ask the children to count all of Jesus' friends.
Note: If you don't have enough children for this activity, follow the instructions above, choosing as many children as you have and let the remainder be pretend people.

Talk About
1. Why did God want us to have friends? Why do you think Jesus wanted to have friends?
2. What do friends do for each other?
3. Can the people in your family be your friends?
4. How do you know when someone is your friend?

Jesus' Life, Death, and Resurrection

The Triumphal Entry
Mark 11:1-10

Materials
- large pieces of green construction paper (one per child)
- pencil
- scissors

Prepare Ahead of Time
- Draw palm leaves on the paper. Cut out the leaves.

While You Tell the Story

Ask the children to pretend to be the crowd that greeted Jesus as he rode toward Jerusalem. Wave the palm branches and shout, "Hosanna to the Son of David! Blessed is he who comes in the name of the Lord!"

Place the palm branches along a pretend pathway for Jesus to ride over. Encourage some of the children to pretend to be riding on the donkey, clip-clopping and bounding back and forth.

As you march and dance and wave your branches, sing this song to the tune of "Three Blind Mice."

> *Hosanna! Hosanna!*
> *Hosanna! Hosanna!*
> *Hear us shout and hear us sing!*
> *Hosanna to our Lord and King!*
> *He's the ruler of everything!*
> *Hosanna! Hosanna!*

Optional: Ask an adult or teen to act as a donkey by dressing in brown, crawling on the floor, and giving each child a donkey ride as the others call "Hosanna!"

Talk About
1. Why were the people excited?
2. Why did God send Jesus to the earth? (Read John 3:16 from a simple version.)
3. How can we praise and worship Jesus now?

Jesus' Life, Death, and Resurrection

Jesus Washes His Friends' Feet
John 13:1-17

Materials
- large bowl or tub of water
- towels

While You Tell the Story

Pretend to be walking on a dirt road. Talk about how dusty, dirty, and tired your feet are getting. Have the children sit down and take off their shoes and socks. Put each child's socks inside his shoes besides where he is sitting. Wash and dry the children's feet as you tell the story. Put their socks and shoes back on.

Talk About
1. Why did Jesus wash his friends' feet?
2. Jesus was serving and helping. How can you serve and help others?

Jesus' Life, Death, and Resurrection

The Lord's Supper
Matthew 26:17-30; 1 Corinthians 11:23-26

Materials
- tablecloth
- paper plates
- small paper cups
- grape drink (like Kool-Aid)
- unleavened bread or matzo crackers

Prepare Ahead of Time
- Mix the grape drink and have it ready to serve in a pitcher.

While You Tell the Story

Lead the children around the room, pretending to look for the special room where Jesus can eat supper with his friends. Pretend to go up, up, up the stairs. Then say, "Here it is! Let's get supper ready."

Spread the tablecloth out on a table or on the floor. The children sit around the table or around the tablecloth on the floor. Give each child a plate and cup. Tell about how Jesus said, "I won't be with you much longer. I'm going back to Heaven soon."

Then pour the grape drink into the cups and give the children some of the unleavened bread. Tell how Jesus said that he was giving them this to help them remember him.

Talk About
1. Have you ever seen anyone else eat something like this? Where?
2. Who does this remind us of? What does it make us think about?
3. This is part of worshiping Jesus. How else can we worship him?

> Jesus' Life, Death, and Resurrection

Jesus' Death and Resurrection
Luke 23:26–24:12; Matthew 27:32–28:10

Materials
- poster board
- scissors
- tape or tacks
- three or four flashlights
- one adult or youth volunteer
- bedsheet

Prepare Ahead of Time
- Cut a cross shape out of the poster board. Place the cross at the front of the room or on a bulletin board.
- Make a cave-like tomb by draping the sheet over some chairs or a table.

While You Tell the Story
   Darken the room. Hold two flashlights. Ask your adult helper to hold one flashlight. Shine all three flashlights on the cross when you tell the part where it says "they crucified him." Then ask your helper to turn off his flashlight when Jesus says, "Forgive them." Turn off the second flashlight when Jesus says, "Today you shall be with me in Paradise." Turn off the third flashlight when Jesus says, "I give my spirit to you." Finish the story. (If necessary, a fourth flashlight can be used to keep some light in the room in case the children are uncomfortable in the darkened room.)
   Tell about how Jesus' body was placed in a cave-like tomb. Shine your flashlights on the cave. Tell how two days passed. Then tell about the women who woke up early in the morning to go to the tomb. Choose two children to go look inside. It's empty! Everyone claps and says, "Jesus is alive!"

Talk About
1. Why did Jesus die?
2. Did Jesus stay dead? What happened to him?
3. Where is Jesus now?

Jesus' Life, Death, and Resurrection

Jesus Meets Friends on the Road to Emmaus
Luke 24:13-35

Materials
- butcher paper
- marker
- crayons
- blocks
- story figures (see appendix A for suggestions)

Prepare Ahead of Time
- Cut a 5-foot length of butcher paper and draw a road down the middle of it.
- Make three story figures.

While You Tell the Story

Roll out the butcher paper "road" on the floor and ask the children to color it. Have them build a block city at each end of the road.

Using the story figures, tell the story. Make the figures walk slowly and sadly down the road to Emmaus and then hurry back the other way to tell how they had seen Jesus.

Talk About
1. Do you ever go for a walk? Where do you like to walk?
2. Whose feet were walking on the road in our story? What happened?
3. How do you show that you're glad Jesus is alive?

Jesus' Life, Death, and Resurrection

Jesus Makes Breakfast for His Friends
John 21:1-14

Materials
- masking tape
- construction paper
- blocks
- pan of cooked fish sticks of fish-shaped crackers
- bedsheet
- scissors
- flashlight

Prepare Ahead of Time
- Cut fish out of construction paper, using the pattern on page 169 in the appendix.
- Bake the fish sticks.
- Put masking tape on the floor in the shape of a boat large enough for the children to sit in.

While You Tell the Story
Let the children get into the boat shape. Give them the sheet to use as a net for fishing. As you tell the story, the children pretend to fish from the boat. They catch no fish at first. Then tell how Jesus told them to throw the net on the other side of the boat. They put the net on the other side. Fill it with the construction paper fish.

Then turn a flashlight on and stack a few blocks over it to make a campfire. Tell how Jesus cooked fish for their breakfast. The children may gather around the campfire and eat the fish sticks you have baked or the fish-shaped crackers.

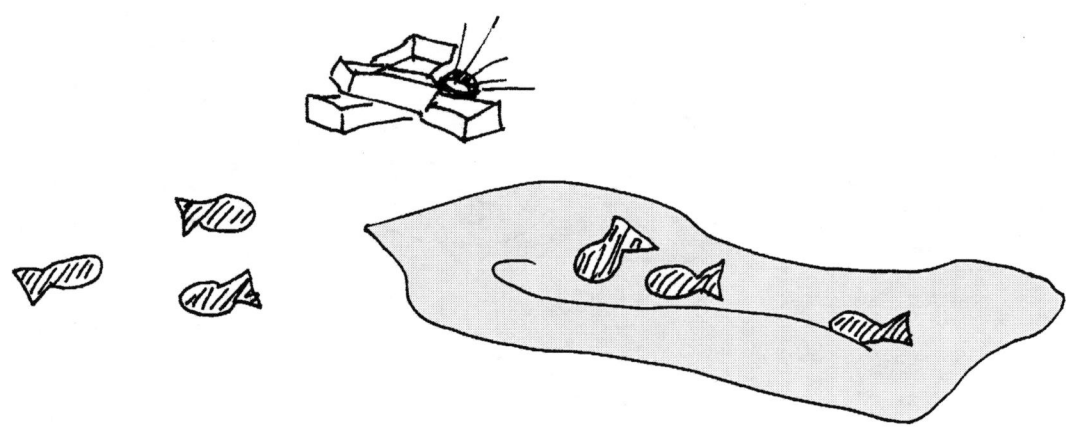

Talk About
1. How did Jesus' friends know that the man on shore was Jesus?
2. How did Jesus help his friends?
3. How does Jesus help you?

Jesus' Life, Death, and Resurrection

Jesus Goes Back to Heaven
Acts 1:6-11

Materials
- two pieces of construction paper
- scissors
- hole punch
- string
- cotton balls or quilt batting
- glue

Prepare Ahead of Time
• Cut a figure out of construction paper as shown on page 170 in the appendix. Punch a hole in the top and tie a 2-foot length of string to it. Cut a cloud out of another piece of construction paper. Glue cotton balls or quilt batting over the cloud shape.
• Punch a hole in the top of the cloud. Tie a long piece of string to the cloud shape. Hang it from the ceiling, light, or door frame until it is about 2 feet from the ground.

While You Tell the Story
    As you tell the story, hold the figure (which represents Jesus) by the string. Gently raise him up behind the cloud as you tell how he ascended. Then hold the string of the cloud. Raise them both as high as you can with Jesus hidden by the cloud. Tell the rest of the story.

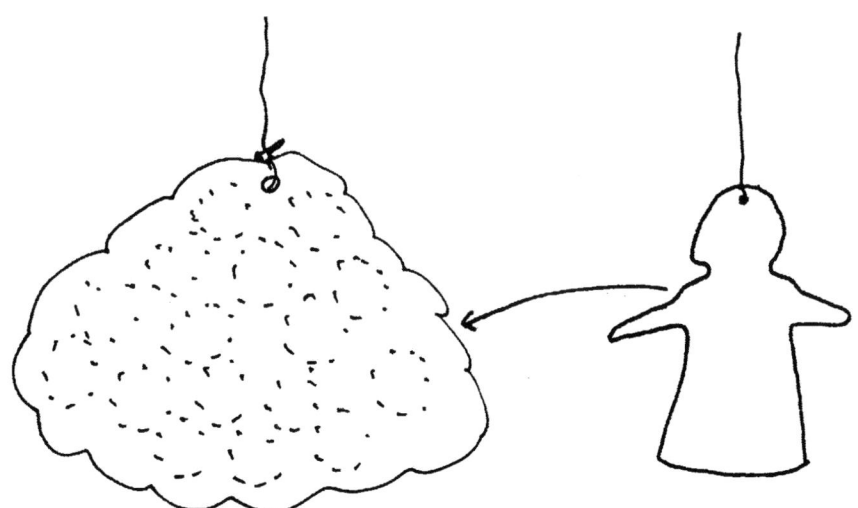

Talk About
1. Why did Jesus go back to Heaven? (He was going home! He would get to see his father again!)
2. How did Jesus' friends feel when they saw Jesus go into the sky?
3. Before Jesus left, what did he tell his friends they would do? Is that something you can do, too? How?

Jesus' Miracles

Water Into Wine
John 2:1-11

Materials
- plastic pitcher
- red powdered drink mix (like Kool-Aid)
- paper cups
- liquid measuring cup
- stirring spoon
- water

Prepare Ahead of Time
• Pour the powdered drink mix into the pitcher. (If the drink mix you have selected needs sugar, add it prior to class.)

While You Tell the Story
Pretend the class is at the wedding. Give each child an empty cup. Pretend everyone has run out of their drinks. Tell them what Jesus did. Let the children see you pouring clear water into the pitcher. Stir it. Fill each child's cup with the drink. Be sure to tell the children how you made the water turn into red Kool-Aid. But tell them that Jesus really made water turn into wine.

Talk About
1. Why did the people need Jesus' help?
2. What did Jesus do? Who knew what really happened?
3. Why do you need Jesus' help? How can you tell him?

Jesus' Miracles

The Great Catch of Fish
Luke 5:1-11

Materials
- paper, poster board, or cardboard
- scissors
- blue bedsheet for the lake
- beach towel or other large towel for the net
- masking tape or blocks for boat

Prepare Ahead of Time
- Cut out fish shapes using the pattern on page 171 in the appendix.
- Make an outline of a boat on the floor with masking tape or blocks. Make it large enough for the children to sit inside.

While You Tell the Story
   Spread out the sheet beside the boat outline. Ask the children to get into the boat. Guide the children in pretending to cast a net (a towel) out of their pretend boat. At first they catch nothing. Then direct them to put the net on the other side. Toss the fish into the towel so the children can pull them into the boat.

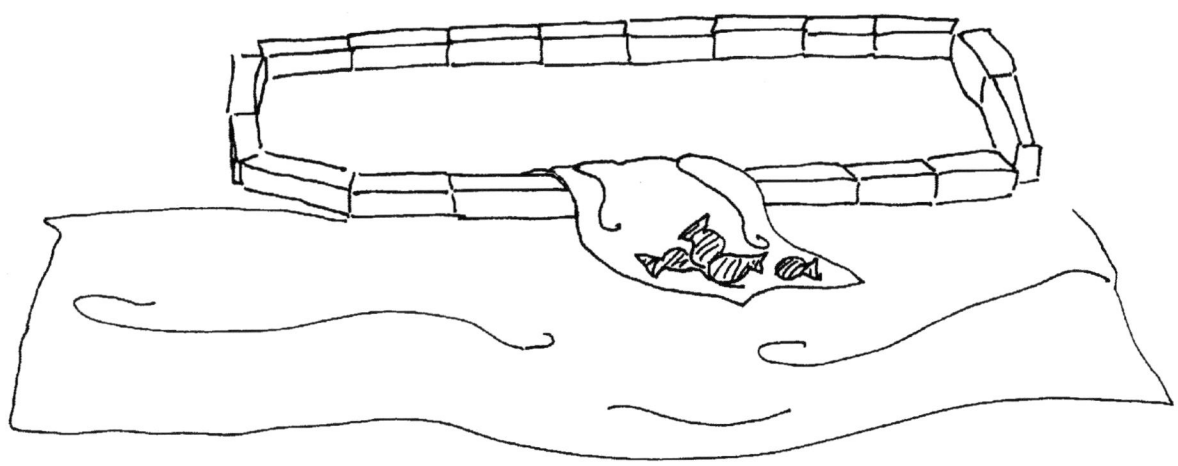

Talk About
1. At first, Jesus' friends didn't catch any fish. They tried and failed. How do we feel when we fail?
2. How did Jesus encourage his friends?
3. Do you know somebody who needs encouraging? How can you encourage them?

> Jesus' Miracles

Peter's Mother-in-Law
Matthew 8:14-17

Materials
• pillow and blanket or quilt

Prepare Ahead of Time
• Ask another adult to act the part of the mother-in-law.
• Rehearse questions that you might ask a sick person, interview-style.

While You Tell the Story
    Let the adult helper lie on the quilt and groan, pretending to be sick. You or another child can interview her for the nightly news while she is sick. Then tell what happened when Jesus got there. Interview her again after she has been made well.

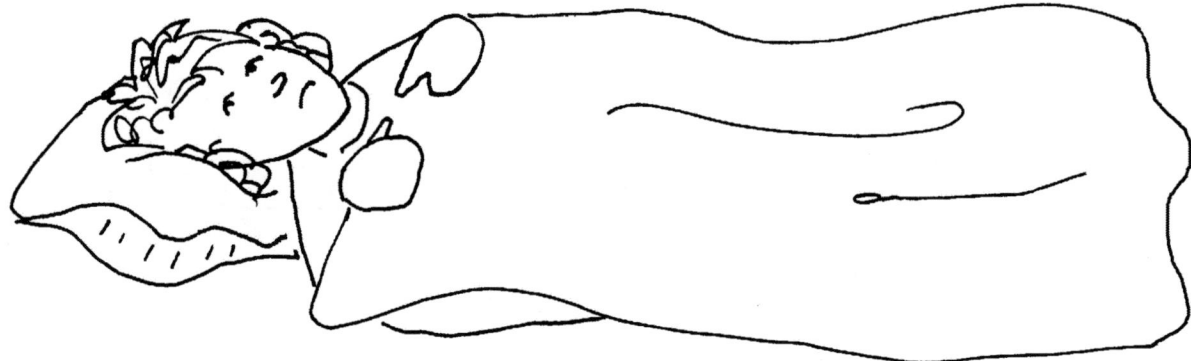

> **Talk About**
> 1. Have you ever been sick? What did you feel like?
> 2. Who took care of you when you were sick?
> 3. What happened to Peter's mother-in-law? What did she do when she got well? After you've been sick and you get well again, how do you feel? Who heals us?

Jesus' Miracles

Through the Roof
Luke 5:17-26

Materials
- shoe box with lid *
- scissors
- toy people or clothespin figures (See appendix A for instructions.)
- a small piece of cloth

Prepare Ahead of Time
- Make a shoe box house. Take the lid off the shoe box, turn the box upside down, cut a square in the roof, and draw or cut out a door and windows. With the lid of the shoe box, cut out a square of cardboard that is a bit larger than the square hole in the roof. Set it over the hole. Cut a small rectangle out of the same cardboard lid. This rectangle must be large enough to hold a figure and small enough to fit through the hole in the roof. Cut a small piece of cloth, as shown, and tie the figure onto the mat with the cloth.

*You can also build the house out of blocks, placing a thin piece of cardboard on top of the block house to make a roof. Cut a hole in the roof with scissors.

While You Tell the Story
Make a crowd of figures around the house. Tell the story using the figures. Carry the cardboard mat to the house. Take the covering off the hole and set the mat down into the house. Tell what happened. When you get the sick man in the house, let each child take a peek through the roof to see him.

Talk About
1. The sick man couldn't move. How did he get to Jesus?
2. The man's friends couldn't get in the house. Did they give up?
3. The sick man had some very good friends. They helped him. How can you help your friends?

Jesus' Miracles

The Lame Man at the Pool
John 5:1-15

Materials
- sponges
- scissors
- spring-type clothespins
- permanent markers
- pan or bowl of water or a water table

Prepare Ahead of Time
- Cut 1-inch circles out of the sponges. Clip one clothespin to each circle. Draw eyes and mouths on the circles. These are the people at the pool.

While You Tell the Story
Designate one of the figures to be the sick man and one to be Jesus. Tell the story, stirring the water with your hand and showing the other figures getting into the water before the sick man can get there. Show how Jesus came and made the sick man well.

Another idea: Spread a blue bedsheet or tablecloth on the floor. Pretend it is the pool. Ask one child to pretend to be the man who can't make it to the water when it moves. Ask the others to watch for the water to move. They pretend they are sick too and the moving water will make them feel better. Gently shake and ruffle the sheet. The children get in the water. Then tell how other people got in before the sick man could get there. Tell how Jesus came and healed him.

Talk About
1. What was the matter with the man at the pool? Why couldn't he get in the pool?
2. Did Jesus care that the man could not walk? What did Jesus do?
3. Does Jesus care when you are sick or hurt?
4. Who is able to heal? What can we do when we are sick? What can we do when others are sick?

Jesus' Miracles

The Man's Withered Hand
Matthew 12:9-14

Materials
- none

While You Tell the Story

Ask the children to make a fist with one hand and keep their hand that way while you tell the story. Tell about the man at the worship house whose hand was crippled. He had still come to worship God. Go to the children with concern and look at their hands as you tell about Jesus answering the Jews' questions. Tell what Jesus said and did. Tell the children to stretch out their hands.

Talk About
1. What do you do with your hands? Could you draw if your hand was withered? Could you hold a spoon or fork? Could you wash your face or brush your teeth?
2. Why didn't the Jews want Jesus to heal the man?
3. Jesus healed the man. Who can heal us when we are sick?

> Jesus' Miracles

The Centurion's Sick Servant
Matthew 8:5-13

Materials
- piece of construction paper for each child
- three story figures (See appendix A for suggestions.)
- crayons or markers

While You Tell the Story
    Ask the children to sit in a large circle. Give each child a piece of construction paper and tell him to lay it in front of him on the floor. Tell the children the papers are their houses. Let them draw rooms and people in their houses. All of the houses make a small town. Keep the papers in front of the children. In one house, place the captain figure and his sick servant. Walk the Jesus figure into the town and tell the story by moving the figures as needed.

Talk About
1. Why did the captain go to see Jesus? When you are sick, how can you go to Jesus? Who asks Jesus to make you well again?
2. Who takes care of you when you are sick? Who can make you well?

Jesus' Miracles

Jesus Stills the Storm
Mark 4:35-41

Materials
- toy boat or a soap boat
- pan with water

Prepare Ahead of Time
- To make a soap boat, attach a triangular sail or paper to a toothpick and stick it into a bar of soap that floats.

While You Tell the Story

Place the boat in a pan of water. Tell how Jesus is sleeping in a boat as his friends ride. Suddenly a storm blows in. One child can switch the room lights off and on to make lightning. Others can drum their fingers on the floor or table to make rain sounds. Others rub their hands together or blow to make it sound windy. Rock the pan back and forth to make waves as you tell the story.

Tell how Jesus' friends woke him up when they started to feel scared about the storm. Tell how Jesus was able to still the storm and his friends were amazed.

Another idea: Make an outline of a boat on the floor with masking tape, making it large enough for the entire group of children to sit inside. Have everyone sit inside the boat. As you tell the story, have the children move around in the boat as if the water is smooth. Then have the children move around as if the waves are making the boat bob up and down.

Talk About
1. Why were Jesus' friends scared?
2. What are some things you are afraid of?
3. What did Jesus' friends do when they were afraid? What do you do when you are afraid?
4. Who took care of Jesus' friends? Who takes care of you?

Jesus' Miracles

Woman Touches Jesus' Hem
Luke 8:42-48

Materials
• none

While You Tell the Story
    Let the children make a crowd. As you tell the story, try to reach through to the child in the center of the crowd. "If I could only reach . . . reach . . . reach . . . and she did!" Tell the rest of the story.

Talk About
1. When Jesus was touched by the woman, what did he feel?
2. When he asked who touched him, what did Peter say? What did the woman do?
3. Did she need to be shy around Jesus? Do we need to be shy or afraid when Jesus is with us?
4. When is Jesus with us? He cares for us.

Jesus' Miracles

Jairus's Daughter
Luke 8:42, 49-56

Materials
- little girl doll with eyes that close when the doll is laid down
- doll bed or a box with a blanket to be the doll's bed

While You Tell the Story

Hold up the doll. Tell how Jairus's daughter got sick and died. Put the doll in the bed. Tell about the father going to get Jesus, and about Jesus coming to the girl's room. Lift up the doll out of bed as Jesus heals her.

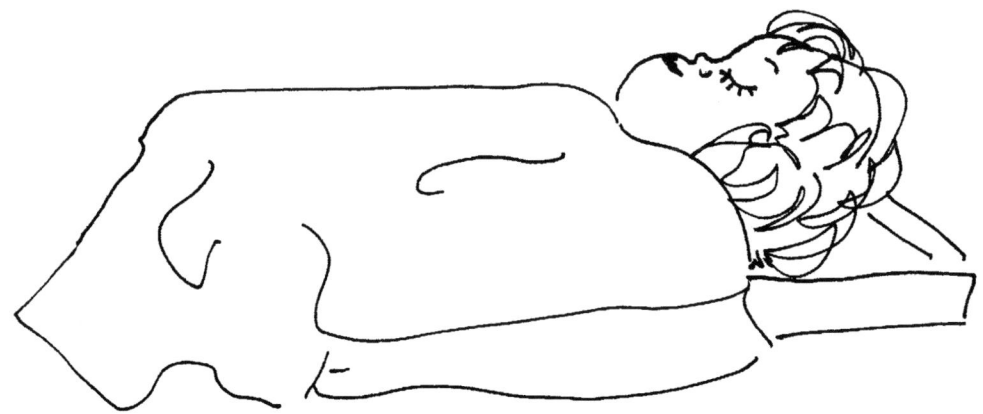

Talk About
1. Does Jesus care about children? Does he care about you?
2. Who prays for you when you get sick?
3. Do you know someone who is sick now? Let's pray for them.

Jesus' Miracles

Jesus Feeds 5,000
Luke 9:10-17

Materials
- basket
- napkins or paper towels
- scissors
- oyster crackers and fish-shaped crackers

Prepare Ahead of Time
• Set aside five oyster crackers and two fish-shaped crackers. Line the bottom of the basket with a paper towel or napkin. Put lots of the oyster crackers and fish crackers on top. Then cover that layer with another paper towel or napkin. On top of that, place the remaining five oyster crackers and two fish-shaped crackers

While You Tell the Story
Ask the children to pretend to be the hungry crowd. Tell how the disciples discussed where to find food for them all. Look around for food. "Discover" the basket. Count the children. Tell the children there were more than 5,000 people. Count the food. Is it enough? Tell how Jesus prayed. Then lift the top layer of crackers and fish and distribute the rest of the crackers so that all of the children have some. They may eat the crackers.

Talk About
1. What did the people need when they got hungry? Did Jesus care that the people were hungry?
2. How does Jesus give food to you? Who makes the food grown in the farmer's field?
3. Does Jesus care about how you feel? How does Jesus take care of you?

Jesus' Miracles

Jesus Walks on Water
Matthew 14:22-33

Materials
- water table or large bowl of water
- small toy figures of Jesus and disciples (See appendix A for suggestions.)
- toy boat or a small bowl to hold the figures

While You Tell the Story
    Tell the story, placing the disciples in the boat or small bowl. Place the boat on the water. Make the boat bob up and down on the waves. The children may be the wind and blow against the boat. Make the Jesus figure walk on the water to the boat as you tell the story.

Another idea: You can also tell the story without the water and still use the figures. You may wish to use a blue bedsheet to represent the lake. You could also use the children instead of story figures. Ask one child to sit at each end of the bedsheet and shake the sheet for gentle waves, harder for stormy waves. Choose one child to be Jesus and one to be Peter. Have the children move to the right places as you tell the story. The other children can pretend to be the disciples in the boat.

Talk About
1. How do you think the disciples felt when the wind was blowing against their boat? How do you think they felt when they saw Jesus on the water?
2. How would you have felt after Jesus was in the boat?
3. When you are in trouble, what do you do? Does Jesus care when you are having problems? How does Jesus help you?

> Jesus' Miracles

Tax Money in a Fish
Matthew 17:24-27

Materials
- construction paper
- dime
- string
- scissors
- clear tape
- magnet
- paper clips
- dowel or stick

Prepare Ahead of Time
• Cut fish shapes out of construction paper (four or five fish will be enough; see the pattern on page 172 in the appendix). Tape a dime to the side of one fish. Clip one paper clip to each fish's mouth.
• Tie a 3-foot piece of string onto the dowel or stick to make a fishing pole.
• Tie a magnet to the other end of the string.

While You Tell the Story
　Tell the story of the men who came to Jesus and Peter and asked about the tax money. When Peter obeys Jesus and goes to catch a fish, choose one child to use the fishing pole and "catch" a fish. Place the fish with the money side next to the floor. When the child catches the fish, he will find money on it. You can put the fish back into the "pond" and let other children go fishing.

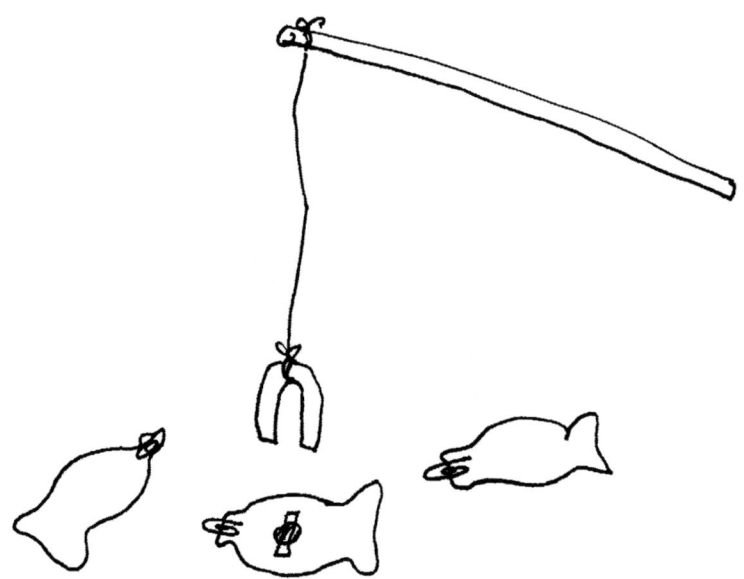

> **Talk About**
> 1. Why did Jesus send Peter to catch a fish? What did Peter find in the fish's mouth?
> 2. Who needs money? Why? How do people get money?
> 3. Does God provide the money we need? How?

Jesus' Miracles

The Ten Lepers
Luke 17:11-19

Materials
- pen

Prepare Ahead of Time
- Draw faces on each of your fingers.
- Practice the finger play so you'll be familiar with it.

While You Tell the Story
Teach the children this finger play.

Ten men were very sad.	(hold up ten fingers)
They were sick and felt so bad.	(frown)
They couldn't even live at home.	(make a house)
They had to live all alone.	
But they saw Jesus walking by.	(make fingers walk)
"Help us, Jesus!" they all cried.	(cup hands at mouth)
Jesus said, "Go home today!"	(point)
And as they all went on their way,	(walk fingers)
One man, two men, three men, four	(hold up fingers)
Saw they were not sick anymore.	
Five, six, seven men, eight, nine, ten	
Ran to get back home again.	(make fingers run)
Then one man stopped and turned around.	(hold up one finger)
He went to Jesus and knelt down.	
He said, "Thank you, Lord, for healing me."	(make praying hands)
And Jesus smiled, for he was pleased.	(smile)

Talk About
1. Why did the men call Jesus to come to them? Why do you need Jesus?
2. How did Jesus help the men? How does Jesus help you?
3. How many men came back to say "thank you"? How do you think that made Jesus feel? What do you need to thank Jesus for?

Jesus' Miracles

Jesus Heals the Bent Woman
Luke 13:10-17

Materials
- none

While You Tell the Story

    Choose one child to be the bent-over woman, and one child to be Jesus. Tell the story in your own words, guiding the children through the appropriate actions. Then choose another child to be the woman, another to be Jesus, and another to tell the story. Take turns as long as the children are interested. If time allows, let all the children try being the bent-over woman and walk around the room.

Talk About
1. Is it hard to walk bent over? Would it be hard to look up into the sky? To get dressed? To play?
2. What was wrong with the lady Jesus saw? How did Jesus help her?
3. How can you help others?

Jesus' Miracles

Blind Bartimaeus
Mark 10:46-52

Materials
- three paper plates
- scissors
- markers
- stapler

Prepare Ahead of Time
- Make a hand puppet from two paper plates, as shown on page 173 in the appendix. First draw the eyes, a nose, and a mouth on one plate. Cut slits about ?-inch-long just above the eyes. On another plate, draw eyelids, as shown. Cut out the eyelids, fringe the lower edges to make eyelashes, fold back the tabs as, as shown, and insert the tabbed end into the slots. Then unfold the tabs to secure the eyelids in place. Staple another paper plate to the first paper plate, leaving the bottom open to make a place for your hand to slip inside.

While You Tell the Story
Tell the story using the paper plate hand puppet with the eyelids closed. When Jesus heals the blind man, take two of your fingers and pull down on the tabbed ends of the eyelids inside the puppet to make the eyes open. Finish the story.

Another idea: Ask the children to close their eyes and cover their eyes with their hands. Explain to them that a blind person cannot see. Ask them to listen for footsteps. Walk across the room so the children can hear your footsteps. Tell how the blind man heard people coming and found out that Jesus was with them. The blind man cried out, "Jesus, please help me!" Ask the children to call out like the man did. Tell them what Jesus and the man said and how Jesus healed the blind man.

Have the children take their hands off their eyes and look around. Have everyone stand up, jump around, and say, "I can see! Thank you, Jesus!"

Talk About
1. What did Bartimaeus want? What did the people tell him? Did he do it?
2. Did Jesus hear Bartimaeus? Did Jesus tell him to be quiet? What did Jesus do for him?
3. Does Jesus hear you? What do you talk to Jesus about? What do you need? How does Jesus help you?

Jesus' Teachings

The Woman at the Well
John 4:1-42

Materials
- chairs; pillows or cushions; or a large, empty box
- bucket, small pail, or small box
- string or rope

Prepare Ahead of Time
- Make a pretend well by putting chairs in a circle, by placing pillows and cushions on top of each other in a circle, or by using the large box.

While You Tell the Story
    Tie a string or rope to the bucket and let it down into the well as you tell the story.

Talk About
1. What is worship? What is praise?
2. When should we worship? Where can we worship? Is it only done when we get together on Sundays?
3. Can we worship when we are having a bad day, or when things are not going well?
4. How can we worship? What is your favorite way to worship?

Jesus' Teachings

Jesus Reads in the Synagogue
Luke 4:16-22

Materials
- several sheets of plain white paper
- tape
- two cardboard paper towel tubes or two unsharpened pencils

Prepare Ahead of Time
- Make a scroll by laying several sheets of the plain white paper next to each other, short ends together. Tape them together to make a long strip of paper. Tape each end of the strip to a cardboard tube or an unsharpened pencil. Roll each end toward the middle to form a scroll.

While You Tell the Story
   Tell how Jesus went to the worship house to read God's words. Tell how Jesus told the people that the words were about him. Tell how the people are amazed to hear him read the words. Let the children take turns pretending to be Jesus reading from the scroll. Have the children repeat some of Isaiah's words after you.

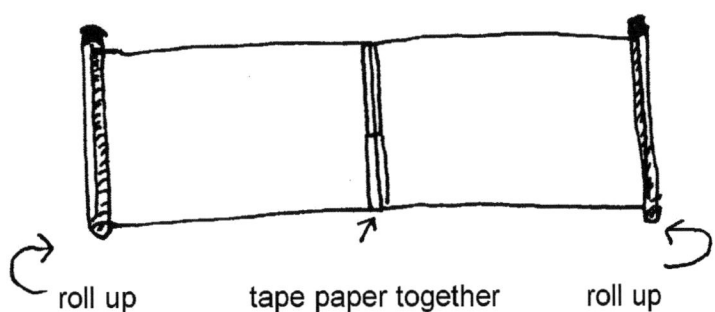
roll up   tape paper together   roll up

Talk About
1. What does our Bible say about God? What else does our Bible tell us?
2. What is your favorite Bible story?
3. What did the people in our story think when they heard Jesus reading God's words?

Jesus' Teachings

Let Your Light Shine
Matthew 5:13-16

Materials
- salt
- candle or flashlight
- paper plate

While You Tell the Story
　　Pour a pile of salt onto the plate as you tell about salt. Turn off the lights and use a candle or flashlight as you tell about light.

Talk About
1. A light helps us see around us. When we do good things, it helps people see what Jesus is like. Salt makes food taste better. The good things we do make people feel better.
2. What are some good things you can do?
3. When you do good things, what does that tell people about Jesus?

Jesus' Teachings

Birds and Flowers
Matthew 6:25-34

Materials
- one paper baking cup per child
- green chenille wires
- play dough
- tape
- reinforcements (for holes of notebook paper)
- tape
- perfume
- paper
- scissors
- string

Prepare Ahead of Time
• Make baking cup flowers. The children can help. Tape a chenille wire onto each baking cup. The cup makes the petals. The wire makes the stem. Put perfume in the center of the flowers.
• Makes birds as shown in the pattern on page 174 in the appendix.

While You Tell the Story
Tell this story outdoors if possible. If you need to be inside, pretend to go for a walk and sit on a hillside. Place the baking cup flowers around the group, sticking them in play dough to stand up. Tell what Jesus said to the people. Fly the paper birds around the group.

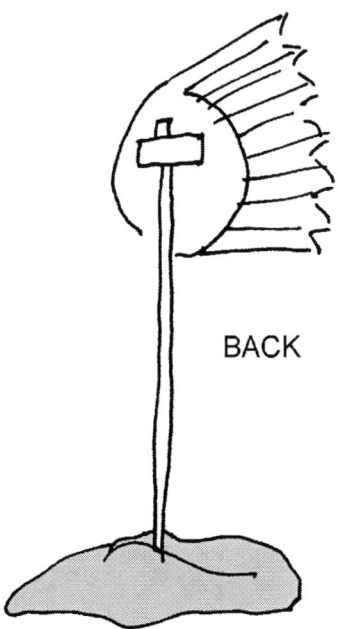
BACK

FRONT

Talk About
1. What did Jesus say about the birds?
2. What did Jesus say about the flowers?
3. Who takes care of birds and flowers? Who takes care of you?

119

Jesus' Teachings

The Lord's Prayer
Matthew 6:5-15

Materials
- five copies of the praying hands pattern on page 175 in the appendix
- copy and cut out the crown, bread, sad face, and one way sign from page 175 in the appendix
- name tag and pen
- tape

Prepare Ahead of Time
• Copy and cut out five praying hands. Copy and cut out the crown, bread, sad face, and one way sign. Place a name tag on the first praying hand. Write *GOD* on it. Put the crown on the next hand, the bread on the next, a sad face on the next, and the one way sign on the last.

While You Tell the Story
  As you tell the Lord's prayer, hang each praying hand on the wall or bulletin board. Talk about what each verse means.
  1. Your name is holy.   (name tag)
  2. Your kingdom come.   (crown)
  3. Give us our daily bread.   (bread)
  4. Forgive us for our sins.   (one sad face)
  5. Lead us not into temptation (one way sign)

Talk About
1. Who prayed in our story? What happened?
2. Where can we pray? When can we pray?
3. What would you like to talk to God about right now? Let's pray together.

Jesus' Teachings

The Wise Man's House
Matthew 7:24-27

Materials
- large rock
- sand
- two plastic or metal bowls or tubs
- play dough
- pitcher of water

Prepare Ahead of Time
- Put sand in one of the tubs. Put the rock in the other.
- Put some water in the pitcher.

While You Tell the Story

Tell the story of the wise man building his house on the rock. Mold a simple house out of the play dough and push it down onto the rock so that it is stuck in place. Tell how the foolish man built his house on sand. Mold a simple house on sand. Tell about the storm that came. Gently pour the water over the house on the rock and the house on the sand. Let the children observe what happens. Compare the house on the rock to listening to God and obeying him. Compare the house on the sand to not listening to God and not obeying him.

Talk About
1. The foolish man does not listen to Jesus. He does not obey. What happened when he had trouble in the big rain?
2. The wise man listens to Jesus. He obeys. What happened when he had trouble in the big rain?
3. What kind of troubles do you have? How can Jesus help you? Do you listen and obey Jesus so he can help you?

Jesus' Teachings

Bigger Barns
Luke 12:13-21

Materials
- large box of oats
- small man figure (See appendix A for suggestions.)
- blocks
- tablecloth or towel

While You Tell the Story

Ask the children to build a small barn for the farmer figure on a tablecloth or towel. Tell the story, taking the roof off the barn and pouring oats into it until it overflows. "He has so much, it won't fit. He can share, but he doesn't."

Ask the children to build a bigger barn. Pour oats into it. "God says the man won't even live long enough to use it all. It would have been better to share."

Talk About
1. How much food did the farmer grow? Could he eat it all?
2. The farmer had a choice: He could keep all his food or share some of it. What did he do? What did God want him to do?
3. What can you share? How does God feel when you share? How do other people feel when you share?

Jesus' Teachings

Sower of Seeds
Matthew 13:1-23

Materials
- paper or plastic cup for each child
- potting soil
- newspaper
- garden trowel or large spoon
- seeds

While You Tell the Story

Tell this story outdoors by a garden, if possible. Ask the children to plant seeds as you tell the story. If you tell it indoors, let the children plant seeds in cups of potting soil as you tell it.

Talk About
1. What happened to the seed on the hard path? Sometimes people act like they are "hard." They don't want to hear about God.
2. Good fruit can grow in a garden. What grows in us when God's Word is in our hearts?

Jesus' Teachings

Hidden Treasures
Matthew 13:44

Materials
- small box with a lid (the kind jewelry comes in)
- yellow construction paper
- hole punch
- sandbox or a shoe box with sand or dirt in it
- plastic spoon or fork
- small man figure (See appendix A for suggestions.)

Prepare Ahead of Time
- Make coins for the treasure chest (the small box) by punching circles out of the yellow paper.
- Bury the treasure chest in the sand or dirt.

While You Tell the Story
    Using the figure, tell how the man went to the field to work. Make the figure dig or rake with the spoon or fork. Then make the figure find the treasure chest and tap on it. Then cover it back up. Tell how the man went and bought the field and dug up the treasure. Emphasize the fact that God's love in our hearts is our treasure.

Talk About
1. What is a treasure? It's something very special to you. You want to keep it and take care of it.
2. What are some treasures (special things) you have at your house?
3. What are some treasures you have in your heart? Why is God's love a special treasure?

> Jesus' Teachings

The Good Samaritan
Luke 10:25-37

Materials
- sandbox
- a few large rocks
- six men figures (See appendix A for suggestions.)
- one donkey figure (See appendix A for suggestions.)

While You Tell the Story

    Let the children help make a road in the sand and set up the rocks. Then using the figures, talk about the man traveling on the road. Show how two robbers jumped out at him, hit him, and took his things. Show the men who came by and would not stop to help. Then show the Samaritan man who came by and did help.

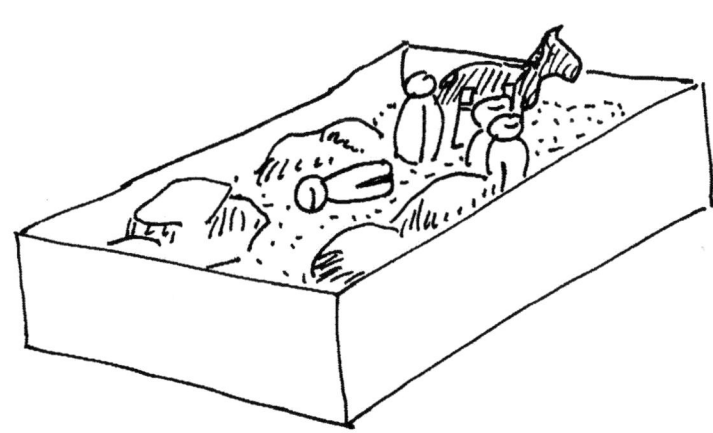

> **Talk About**
> 1. How do you think the hurt man felt when the people didn't help him? Why didn't they help him?
> 2. Who finally helped the man? How did he help?
> 3. Do you know someone who needs your help? How can you help?

Jesus' Teachings

Mary and Martha
Luke 10:38-42

Materials
- none

While You Tell the Story

Together, the children will act out Martha and Mary. Tell about Jesus' coming to Mary and Martha's house.

Ask the children to stand up and mime different jobs as you say them. Quickly say, "Martha sweeps, sweeps, sweeps." The children must sit down. Then slowly say, "Mary listens." The children must sit down and fold their hands in their laps. Quickly say, "Martha dusts, dusts, dusts." The children mime. Slowly say, "Mary listens." The children must sit down and fold their hands in their laps. Do this again and again with different jobs: stir, scrub, chop, pour, wash. At last, tell how Martha complained and what Jesus said.

MARY

MARTHA

Talk About
1. Why did Martha get upset? Who needs your help?
2. What did Jesus say to Martha? Do you ever get upset about anything? How does it feel?
3. What did Jesus say was the best thing to do? The next time you are upset, can you stop and spend some time with Jesus? How?

Jesus' Teachings

The Lost Sheep
Luke 15:3-7

Materials
- one hundred cotton balls
- shoe box lid or blocks

Prepare Ahead of Time
- Hide one of the cotton balls somewhere in the room where the children can find it without too much trouble.

While You Tell the Story
   The children are the shepherds. The cotton balls are their sheep. The shoe box lid is the sheep fold or ask the children to build a fence for the sheep with blocks. Give each child a few cotton balls. Tell the children that all together they should have one hundred sheep. Everyone counts the sheep as you put them into the fold for the night. You should end up with only ninety-nine sheep. The children may hunt for the hidden sheep. You may tell them when they are close (hot) and when they are far away (cold) from the sheep you have hidden. You may want to play this game again by choosing one child to hide the sheep and letting the others search for it.

Talk About
1. How did the shepherd feel when one of his sheep was lost? Do you suppose the sheep got lost because it didn't obey the shepherd, and it didn't come when he called?
2. How does God feel when one of us doesn't obey him?
3. How did the shepherd feel when he found his lost sheep? How does God feel when we decide to obey him?

Jesus' Teachings

The Lost Coin
Luke 15:8-10

Materials
- ten nickels or play coins
- flashlight
- broom

Prepare Ahead of Time
- Hide one of the coins in the room.

While You Tell the Story

Choose one of the children to be the woman in the story. Tell the children that she had ten coins. Give the child the coins and let her count them. She should have only nine. Let her hunt for the hidden coin. She may use the flashlight and sweep under the table and chairs. When she finds it, everyone should rejoice with her by clapping. Then choose another child to be the woman with the coins. The child who found the hidden coin may hide it again, and the new woman can hunt for it as before.

Talk About
1. Did you ever lose something? How does it feel to lose something? How did the lady feel when she lost her coin?
2. How does God feel when people don't obey him?
3. How did the lady feel when she found her coin? How does God feel when people obey him? How can you obey God?

Jesus' Teachings

The Runaway Son
Luke 15:11-24

Materials
- blocks
- small box with a lid (the kind jewelry comes in)
- yellow construction paper
- hole punch
- story figures of an older man and a younger man (See appendix A for suggestions.)

Prepare Ahead of Time
- Make coins to put in the small box by punching holes in the yellow paper. Put the circles of paper in the box.

While You Tell the Story

Let the children build a city with the blocks. Let them build a house some distance away from the city. Moving the figures at the appropriate time, show the children how the son took the money his father gave him and went to a distance city. Tell the children that there he bought what he wanted, went where he wanted, did what he wanted. Out of the box, take a few coins for the clothes he bought. Take a few coins for the food he bought for himself and his friends. Spend the coins until the box is empty. Turn it over and show the children that there was no more money. Finish the story with the young man going home, the father greeting him, and forgiving him.

Talk About
1. How did the father feel when his son left? How does God feel when we don't obey him?
2. What happened to the son in the faraway land? Did he get into trouble? What happens to people when they stop following, loving, and obeying God? (They get into trouble.)
3. Did the father let the son come home? How did the father feel? Does God let people come back and love him again? How does God feel when people start loving him again?

Jesus' Teachings

The Pharisee and a Tax Collector Pray
Luke 18:9-14

Materials
- four paper plates
- stapler
- markers

Prepare Ahead of Time
- Make two puppets by stapling two paper plates together for each puppet, leaving a space to put your hand in between the two plates. Draw a proud face on one and a humble, prayerful face on the other.

While You Tell the Story
Use the paper plate puppets to tell the story.

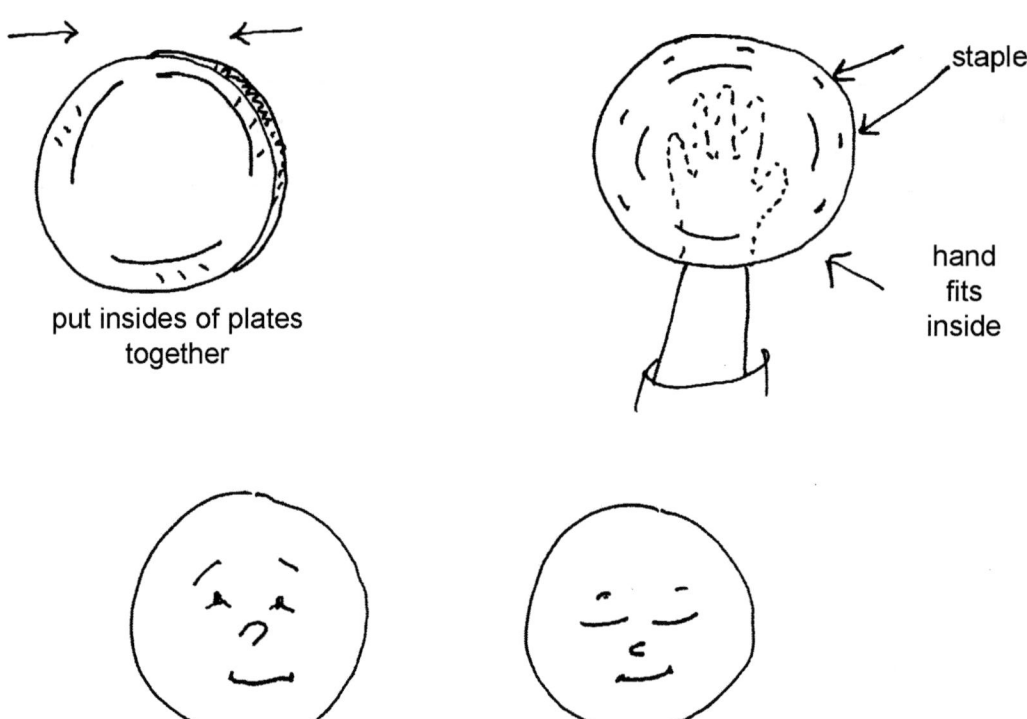

Talk About
1. What was the difference between the prayer of the Pharisee and the prayer of the tax collector?
2. What are some things you know you want? What are some things you know God wants?
3. Can we pray for what God wants? How?

> Jesus' Teachings

Jesus and the Children
Luke 18:15-17; Mark 10:13-16

Materials
- piece of red construction paper
- marker

Prepare Ahead of Time
- Make a stop sign by writing *STOP* on the red paper.
- Ask an adult to act the part of Jesus. Tell him that his job is to say, "Don't stop the children. Let them come to me." Then he and the children will have a group hug.

While You Tell the Story
Give one child the stop sign. Ask the person who is Jesus to sit at the side of the room. The child with the stop sign has the job of holding it out and saying, "Stop!" to any child who comes near Jesus. Lead the rest of the children in skipping and dancing around the room. Sing a song to the tune of "London Bridge."

We are going to see Jesus, see Jesus, see Jesus.
We are going to see Jesus. We're so happy!

Every time the children come close to Jesus, the child with the stop sign stops them. After a few times of this, sit down with the children and look sad. Tell how Jesus' disciples stopped the children. Then the adult portraying Jesus should say his lines. Lead the children to him and have a group hug. Finish the story.

Another idea: Show the children how to use their index finger and middle finger to "walk" them like legs. The children pretend their fingers are the children, walking and jumping, excited to see Jesus. Use fingers on one of your hands to be the disciples who stop the children. Use the fingers on your other hand to be Jesus who tells the children to come. "Hug" the children's fingers with your hand as you tell about how Jesus took the children into his arms.

Talk About
1. Why couldn't the children see Jesus? How do you think they felt?
2. Was Jesus too busy to be with the children? What did he say about it?
3. Is Jesus too busy to be with you now? How can you be with Jesus?

Jesus' Teachings

Zaccaeus
Luke 19:1-10

Materials
• two small, leafy branches, or leaves cut from construction paper (See pattern on page 176 in the appendix.)

Prepare Ahead of Time
• Ask an adult to be the tree. The adult can dress in green.

While You Tell the Story
    Ask your adult tree helper to stay in front of the group and hold a small leafy tree branch in each hand. Let the children stand in front of him. Choose the shortest child to be Zacchaeus. Tell the story. Lead Zacchaeus behind the other children. Ask him to jump up to try to see over everyone. When it's time for Zacchaeus to climb into the tree, ask the tree helper to pick up Zacchaeus. Tell the rest of the story.

Talk About
1. Why did Zacchaeus climb into the tree? What do you think he could see up there?
2. Nobody liked Zacchaeus. Nobody helped him. Why did Jesus talk to him?
3. How did Jesus feel about Zacchaeus? How does Jesus feel about you? Does Jesus want to be with you too? How can Jesus be with you? How can you talk with him?

Jesus' Teachings

Perfume on Jesus' Feet
John 12:1-8

Materials
• perfume

While You Tell the Story
Choose one child to be Mary and one child to be Jesus. Let Jesus take off his shoes. As you tell the story of Mary anointing Jesus' feet with perfume, guide the child who is pretending to be Mary to put a little perfume on the other child's feet. Talk about what this meant, and how we worship Jesus now. You may want to let the children take turns pretending to be Mary and Jesus.

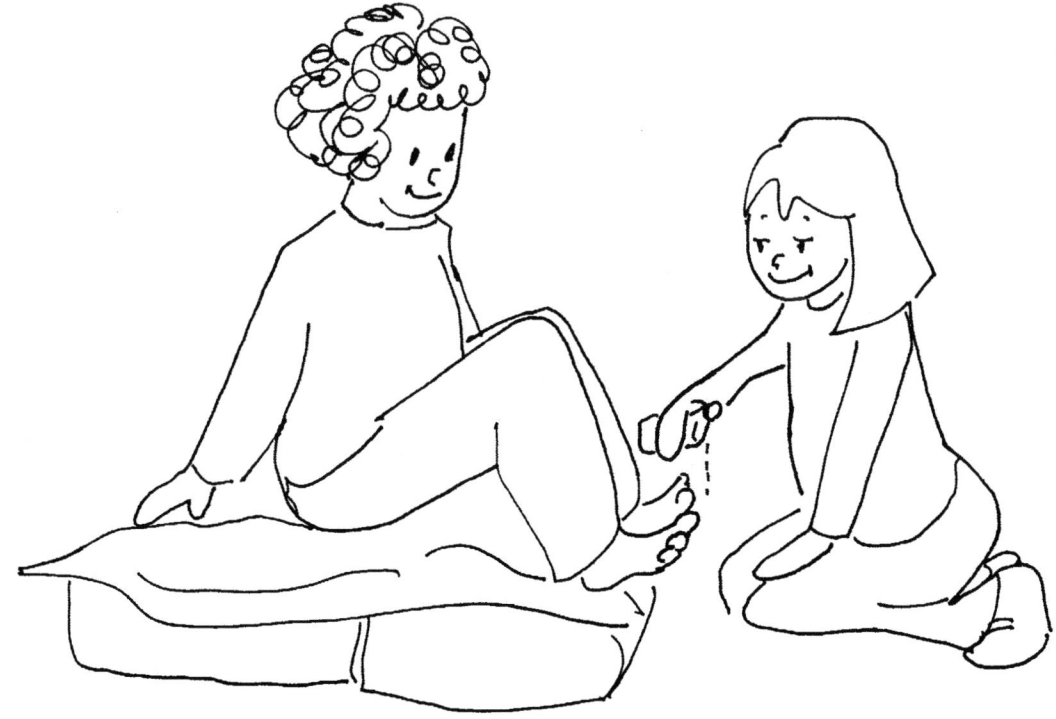

Talk About
1. Why do you think Mary put perfume on Jesus' feet?
2. What is worship? How can you worship Jesus?

> Jesus' Teachings

Two Sons and a Vineyard
Matthew 21:28-31

Materials
- tray or shallow box
- figures of a man, two sons
- leaves (real or cut from construction paper)

While You Tell the Story

Fill the tray or shallow box with leaves. Use the figures to tell the children about a man who had a garden. Ask if they know anyone who has a garden. Talk about how a garden has to have somebody to take care of it.

Then tell about the man and his two sons. Ask which son obeyed.

Another idea: Bring a bunch of grapes. Talk about gardens and vineyards. Let the children tell you what kind of work people have to do to grow food in a garden (plant, water, weed, try to keep bugs off, pick the fruit). Turn two paper cups upside down. Draw a frowning face on one and a smiling face on the other. Place the grapes in one spot to represent the vineyard. Tell the story, moving the frowning cup (the boy who said no) into the vineyard and the smiling cup (the boy who said yes) away from the vineyard. Ask, "Which one obeyed?" Ask, "Which one probably ended up smiling?" The one who obeyed.

> **Talk About**
> 1. What does it mean to obey? What can you do with you hands to help your mother? What can you do with your feet? Mouth? Eyes? Do they help and obey?
> 2. How do you think the father felt when his second son didn't obey? How do you think the father felt when his first son did obey? How does God feel when we obey him?
> 3. How can we obey God? Who else should we obey?

Jesus' Teachings

The Widow's Mite
Mark 12:41-44

Materials
- box with a lid
- scissors
- play money coins or circles of yellow construction paper
- two paper lunch bags

Prepare Ahead of Time
- Put two play money coins into one lunch bag. Put the rest of the coins into the other lunch bag.
- Cut a slot in the lid of the box so the coins can be dropped into the box.

While You Tell the Story
Tell about Jesus being in the temple one day when he saw rich people putting their money into the money box. Choose one of the children to be a rich man. Let him take the sack with a lot of money in it. He chooses two of the coins and puts them into the money box. Tell about the poor woman who brought her money to the temple. Choose one of the children to be the poor woman. Give her the other bag. She takes her two coins and puts them into the money box. Let both children sit down and show what they have left in their bags.

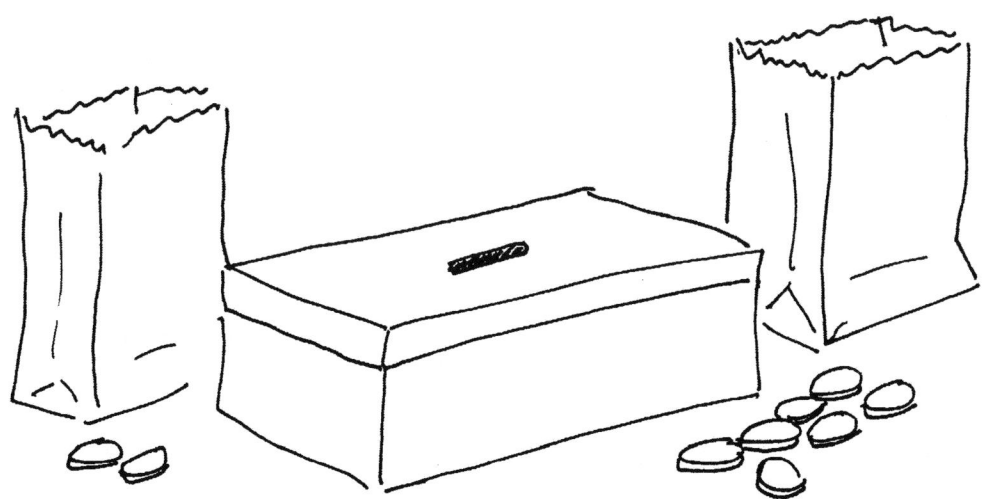

Talk About
1. Which person in our story gave everything?
2. Why do you think the lady gave everything to God?
3. Why do we give money at church? What can you give to God?

The Church

Peter and John Heal a Lame Man
Acts 3:1-10

Materials
- four large pieces of construction paper
- reinforcements (for notebook paper holes)
- scissors
- glue or tape
- markers
- string

Prepare Ahead of Time
- Out of three pieces of construction paper, cut the bodies of Peter, John, and the lame man. Fold the legs accordion-style. See the patterns on page 177 in the appendix.
- Out of the fourth piece of construction paper, cut three circles, each about 3 inches in diameter. Draw eyes, a nose, and a mouth on each. Glue or tape the round heads to the bodies as shown.
- Punch a hole in the tops of the heads. Put reinforcements around the hole, and tie a 36-inch length of string through each.

While You Tell the Story
Make the lame man figure sit on the floor. Holding the other two figures by the strings, walk them toward the lame man as you tell the story of Peter and John going to the temple to pray. When you get to the part of the story where Peter heals the man, pull the lame man figure up by the string and make him walk and jump and praise God.

Another idea: Tell the children to follow you as you walk around the room. Pretend that you are going to the temple to pray. Ask one child to pretend that he can't walk. Give him a place to sit. Tell him to ask for money. Continue walking around as you tell about Peter and John going to pray. Come to the lame man. Tell what Peter told him. Then tell how Peter took the man by the hand and helped him up. Lead all the children in walking and leaping and praising God.

Talk About
1. What did the lame man ask for? How do you think he felt when he was healed?
2. What did the lame man do after he was healed?
3. What do you praise God for? How can you praise God?

The Church

Philip and the Man From Ethiopia
Acts 8:26-40

Materials
- poster board
- marker
- scissors

Prepare Ahead of Time
- Make a floor puzzle by drawing on one side of the poster board a picture of the Ethiopian rejoicing as shown (See instructions for floor puzzle on page 178 in the appendix.) Then turn the poster board over and divide it into twelve sections with a marker. Number each section from 1 to 12, beginning in the top left-hand corner. Draw pictures as shown in the sections and cut the poster board into the sections you have drawn.

While You Tell the Story

Mix up the poster board sections and hand them out to the children. As you tell the story, stop and tell a child with a certain section to place his piece of the puzzle on the floor with the number facing up. For example, "An angel from God came to Philip with a message." The person with the angel may put his square on the floor. "The message said that Philip was to go to a desert road." The person with the road may put his square on the floor next to the angel. Continue in this way, matching these parts of the story and the pictures.

Puzzle Piece Descriptions

1. An angel from God came to Philip with a message (angel).	7. Philip heard him reading (ear).
2. The message said that Philip was to go to a desert road (road).	8. Philip and the man sat down together (sitting figure).
3. Philip saw the Ethiopian man (man's face).	9. The man asked Philip questions (question mark).
4. He was riding in a chariot (chariot).	10. Philip told him about Jesus (word *Jesus*).
5. He was reading from a book of the Bible (book).	11. The man said, "Here is water" (water).
6. Philip ran over to him (running figure).	12. "I want to be baptized" (man in water).

After all of the cards are laid down, turn them over to see a picture of the Ethiopian man rejoicing.

Talk About
1. What was the man in the chariot trying to do?
2. What did Philip do to help the man in the chariot?
3. Can you tell people about Jesus? How? Who do you know who needs to know about Jesus?

The Church

Paul to Damascus
Acts 9:1-19

Materials
- large piece of yellow construction paper
- scissors
- flashlight
- clothespin figures of Saul, his men, and Ananias (See appendix A for instructions.)
- sand table or box of sand

Prepare Ahead of Time
- Cut a large sun shape out of the yellow construction paper.
- Make clothespin figures of Saul, his men, and Ananias.

While You Tell the Story
   Tell the story using the sandbox as the terrain over which the clothespin figures travel. When the bright light shines, let one child hold up the sun. Let another child shine the flashlight on it.

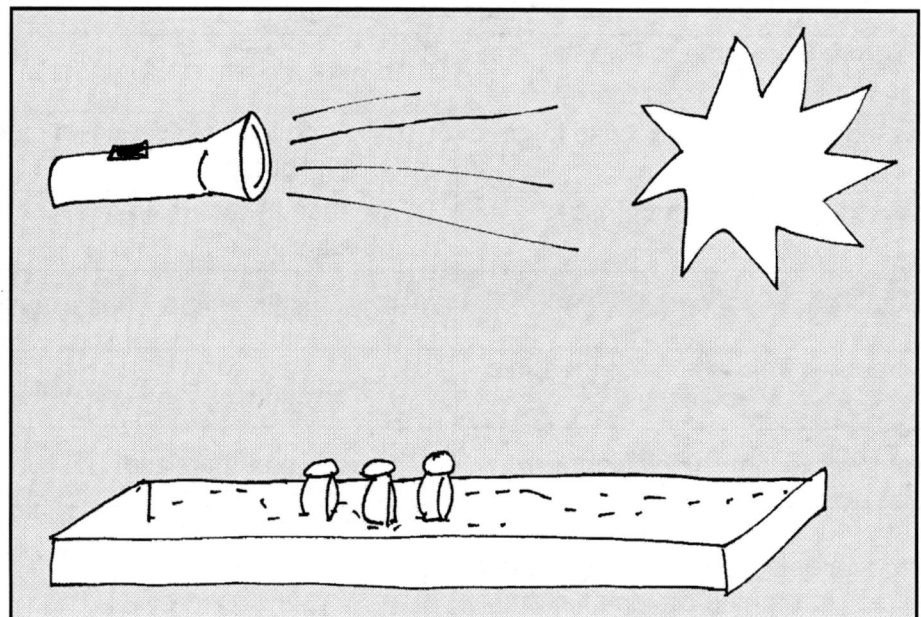

Talk About
1. What was Saul going to do in Damascus? Why did he change his mind?
2. How did Jesus come to him? Why did Jesus choose him?
3. Do you think Jesus has chosen you for something?

The Church

Paul in a Basket
Acts 9:23-25; 2 Corinthians 11:32-33

Materials
- large box or a sheet draped over two chairs
- string
- small basket
- story figure (See appendix A for suggestions.)

Prepare Ahead of Time
- Attach about 18 inches of string to the basket handle.

While You Tell the Story
   Tell this story, setting the large box upright to represent the walls of the city (or the sheet draped over two chairs). Place the Paul figure in the basket, and lower him down slowly over the wall to the outside of the box. Tell how cities used to have walls around them and people went in and out through a gate. Tell how at night they would close the gate to stay safe.

Talk About
1. Why did Paul have to get out of the city? Why did he have to go in a basket?
2. Who helped Paul get away?
3. How do your friends help you? How do you help your friends?

139

The Church

Paul and Barnabas
Acts 9:26-27; 13:2-4

Materials
- four paper plates
- pen or marker

Prepare Ahead of Time
- On paper plates, draw faces with different expressions (as shown): joyful; fearful; mouth open as if talking; praying.

While You Tell the Story
   Hold up the paper plates as you tell the story. Paul was joyful. The people were fearful. Barnabas told them Paul was a good person. Barnabas was being a good friend for Paul. The people became joyful. The leaders were praying. God told them to send Paul and Barnabas to other lands to tell people about Jesus. So they sent Paul and Barnabas. Paul and Barnabas were good friends. They helped each other.

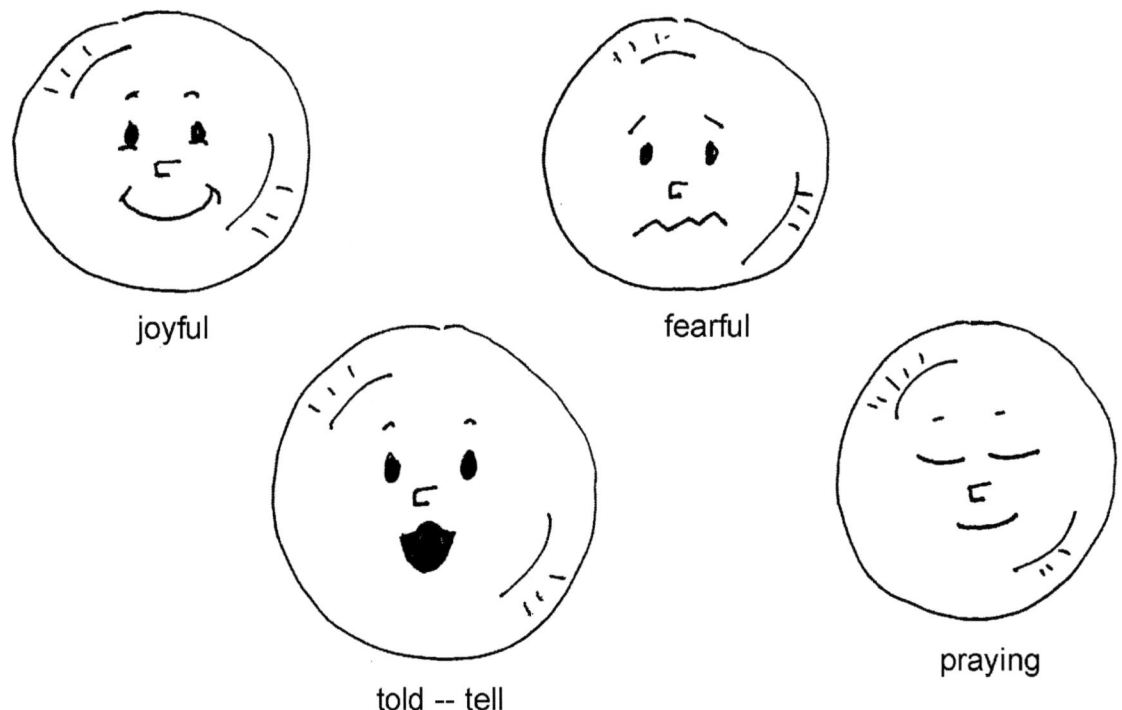

joyful　　　　fearful

told -- tell　　　　praying

Talk About
1. How do friends act toward each other?
2. What do you like to do with your friends? Who gives us friends?
3. Who were friends in our story? What happened?

The Church

Dorcas
Acts 9:36-43

Materials
- two pieces of poster board, different colors
- scissors
- marker

Prepare Ahead of Time
- Make a weaving of poster board by cutting one of the pieces of poster board width-wise into fourteen 2-inch strips. Cut 26-inch slits every 2 inches lengthwise in the other piece of poster board. Weave the 2-inch strips into the slits of the other posterboard as shown. Then using the marker, draw a simple smiling Dorcas figure. Number the strips from top to bottom in order, and then remove them.

While You Tell the Story
Give each child a 2-inch strip of the poster board weaving. Tell the story, stopping now and then to let each child, in order of their strip numbers, weave in his strip. When the story and the weaving are finished, the children will be able to see the smiling Dorcas.

Another idea: Seat the children in a circle. One child lies in the middle to be Dorcas. Give the other children shirts to show what Dorcas gave them, or let them point to their own clothes. Ask the children to pretend to pray like Peter did. Then Dorcas can sit up, alive!

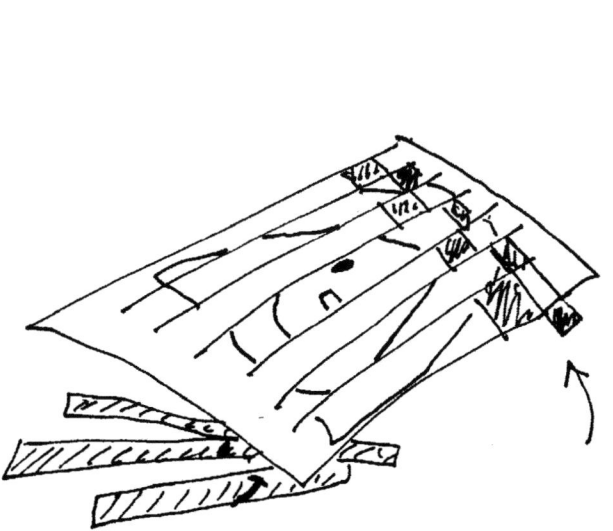

Talk About
1. How did Dorcas help the people she knew?
2. How did God help Dorcas?
3. How does God help you?

141

The Church

Peter and Cornelius
Acts 10

Materials
• bedsheet
• variety of stuffed animals

Prepare Ahead of Time
• Fill the bedsheet with stuffed animals.

While You Tell the Story
    Tell about Peter's dream. Tell how he didn't want to eat because those animals were different than what he usually ate. Open the bedsheet and look at all the stuffed animals. Tell how Cornelius was different than Peter and how they became friends.

Talk About
1. Who are some of your friends? How do we treat friends?
2. What do you like to do with your friends? Who gives us good friends?
3. Who were the friends in our story?

The Church

Peter Escapes From Prison
Acts 12:1-19

Materials
- ten index cards
- glue
- ten balloons
- string
- hole punch
- marker

Prepare Ahead of Time
- Copy and cut out the pictures on pages 179 in the appendix. Glue each one onto an index card. Punch a hole in the top of each card. Put one end of a 36-inch string into the hole of each index card and tie it securely.
- Blow up the balloons. Tie the other end of each string to a balloon. Mark each balloon with a number, 1 through 10.

While You Tell the Story
Tell the story by letting one child find the balloon marked with a 1. Display the picture at the end of it's string. Read and tell what happened. Then let another child find the balloon marked with a 2. Show the picture and read what happened. Continue in this way through the tenth balloon and picture.

Another idea: Create a jail out of chairs by placing the chairs side-by-side in a square or circle, seats facing out. Choose a child to be Peter and have him lie down in the jail. Talk about Peter spending the night in jail. The teacher pretends to be the angel. The child should do what the angel says and follow the angel out of the jail. When you say the angel disappeared, then ask, "Where should we go? It's night. I know! The best place to go is to Rhoda's house. Friends are there." Pretend to go through the streets and knock on Rhoda's door. Finish telling the story. If time allows, let each child take a turn being Peter in jail.

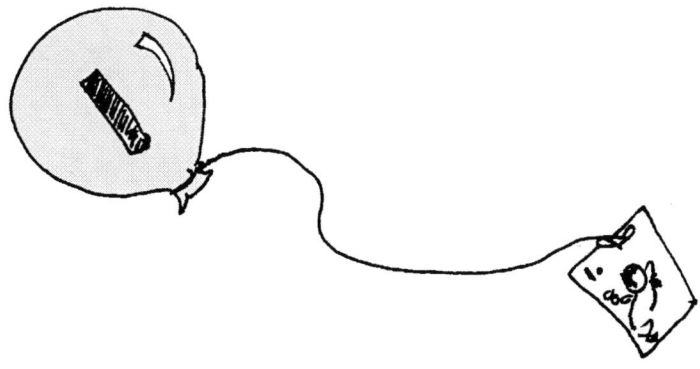

Talk About
1. Why was Peter in prison? What were his friends doing?
2. Did God hear Peter and his friends praying? Does God hear your prayers?
3. How did God answer their prayers? How did God take care of Peter? How does God take care of you?

The Church

Paul in Lystra
Acts 14:8-18

Materials
- chenille wires
- clay or Styrofoam plates
- colored tissue paper
- blocks (optional)

Prepare Ahead of Time
- Make chenille wire people for Paul, Barnabas, the crippled man, and some for the crowd. (See appendix A for instructions.)
- Tear and crumple small pieces of tissue paper to make flowers.

While You Tell the Story
    You may want to let the children build a city. Move the figures as needed, standing them up by sticking the wire into clay or into a Styrofoam plate turned upside down. When the people prepare to worship Paul and Barnabas, sprinkle the tissue flowers at the city gate or near the Paul and Barnabas figures. Finish telling the story.

Talk About
1. What did Paul do for the crippled man?
2. What did all the people of the city do? Paul and Barnabas could have been famous and pretended to be important gods. But what did they do instead? Why?
3. What did Paul tell the people? Can you tell people about God? How?

> The Church

Timothy

Acts 16:1-2; Philippians 2:22
1 Thessalonians 3:6; 2 Timothy 1:5

Materials
- two women figures, two men figures (See appendix A for suggestions.)
- blue bedsheet
- one piece of construction paper for each child, any color
- one piece of brown construction paper
- scissors
- stapler

Prepare Ahead of Time
- Make a boat by cutting the brown paper in half to make two 9-by-6-inch pieces. Cut as shown below. Bring the sides up and fold the tabs in. Staple to secure.

While You Tell the Story
Stretch out the blue sheet to make the sea. Seat the children around the sheet. Give each child a piece of construction paper to put at the edge of the sheet. Tell them these are different cities. Place the two women figures and one man figure on one paper. These are Timothy, his mother, and grandmother. Tell about their faith and how Paul met Timothy and asked Timothy to travel with him. Put them in a boat and sail them across the sea to different places. Then leave Paul in one place and tell how Timothy took messages from Paul to other places. Timothy and Paul became such good friends that they were almost like family to each other.

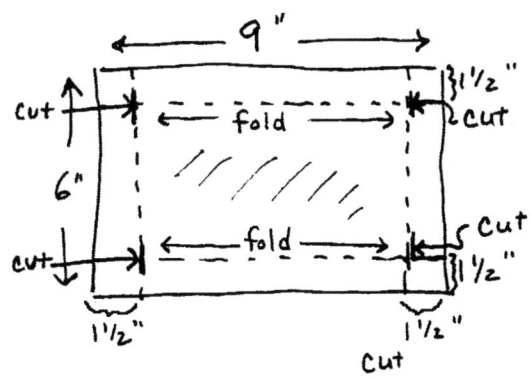 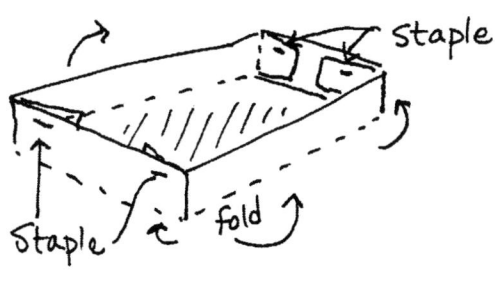

> **Talk About**
> 1. Paul and Timothy became very good friends. Who are your very good friends?
> 2. Timothy's mother and grandmother taught him about Jesus. How does your family help you learn about Jesus?
> 3. Timothy helped Paul. How do you help your friends and family?

The Church

Lydia
Acts 16:11-15

Materials
• blue bedsheet or tablecloth

While You Tell the Story
   Stretch out the blue sheet on the floor to make a river. Choose one child to be Paul and one to be Lydia. Ask the children to help you sing and pray as if you are Lydia and her friends. Move Paul into the group as you tell the story. Tell how Paul goes to the river to find a place to pray. Tell how Paul finds Lydia and some women there and talks to them about Jesus. Tell how Lydia believed Paul, was baptized, and asked Paul to come stay at her house.

Talk About
1. How can you be kind to friends?
2. Who were the friends in our story? How were they kind to each other?

The Church

Paul and Silas in Prison
Acts 16:16-35

Materials
- two men figures (See appendix A for suggestions.)
- large piece of black construction paper
- scissors
- stapler
- tablecloth or bedsheet

Prepare Ahead of Time
- Fold the construction paper in half lengthwise as shown, and cut slits from the folded side to within 1-inch of the edge. Open the paper and curve it around until the short edges overlap. Staple the short edges together. This becomes the jail.

While You Tell the Story
  Place the tablecloth or sheet on the floor. Set the jail on top of it. Tell the story, placing the two figures, Paul and Silas, inside the jail. When the earthquake happens, let the children hold onto the edges of the tablecloth or sheet and shake it. The jail will fall, and you can bring Paul and Silas out. Tell the rest of the story.

Another idea: Mail jail bars by cutting five 3-foot lengths of 1 1/2 inch wide black cloth ribbon. Lay one end of each ribbon piece on top of a 2-foot long dowel. The ribbons should be spaced apart like jail bars. Tape the ends to the dowel with black electrical tape. Tape the other ends to another dowel. Hold up the jail bars as if the children are behind them. Sing together. Then pat the floor to make an earthquake rumble. Shake the bars and then drop them. Tell the rest of the story.

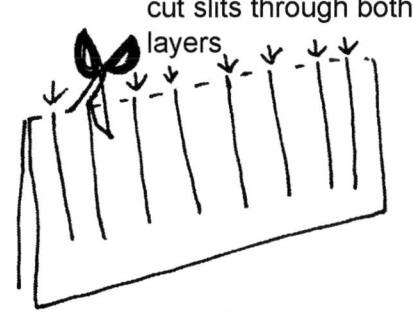
cut slits through both layers

- open out
- curve

staple

Talk About
1. What did Paul and Silas do in jail? Did God hear them?
2. When can you pray and sing to God? Does God hear you anywhere you are?
3. How did God help Paul and Silas? How did Paul and Silas treat the jailer who had locked them up? Why were they nice to him?

The Church

Paul's Nephew Hears a Plot
Acts 23:12-35

Materials
- blocks
- three or four flashlights

While You Tell the Story

Stack the blocks up to make a campfire. Put the flashlights among the blocks and turn them on. Turn off the lights in the room and cover the windows if it's light outside. Begin telling the story. When you tell about the seventy horsemen and the other soldiers taking Paul out of the city, take one of the flashlights yourself and give the others to some of the children. Lead everyone in pretending to gallop away with Paul.

Talk About
1. What did Paul's nephew hear?
2. How did Paul's nephew show that he was brave?
3. What does it mean to be brave? How can you be brave?
4. Paul's nephew helped Paul by telling what he heard. How can you help your family?

The Church

Paul's Shipwreck
Acts 27:13-44

Materials
- blue bedsheets
- blocks

Prepare Ahead of Time
• Let the children help make the outline of a boat using blocks. Make it big enough for the children to get in. Lay the sheets on the floor outside of the boat.

While You Tell the Story
   Tell the story with the children in the boat outline. Hold the edges of the sheet and billow it up and down to make waves. Ask the children to rock back and forth as you tell the story. Tell how the ship broke apart and ask them to swim off the sheet onto the shore.

Talk About
1. Why was Paul brave on the ship?
2. Who helped Paul get through all of his troubles? Who helps you through all of your troubles?
3. Paul even thanked God when the ship was tossing in the sea. He thanked God for the food they ate. Can you thank God too, even in times of trouble?

The Church

Paul on Malta
Acts 28:1-10

Materials
- blocks
- construction paper
- scissors
- flashlight

Prepare Ahead of Time
- Make a paper snake by cutting a spiral.

While You Tell the Story
    Have the children help you build a "campfire" out of blocks stacked like wood. Put a flashlight in the block stack. Turn off or dim the lights. Tell how winter was coming. Tell the story, asking the children to rub their arms and shiver. When you tell about the snake, pull out the paper snake. Tell how God took care of Paul.

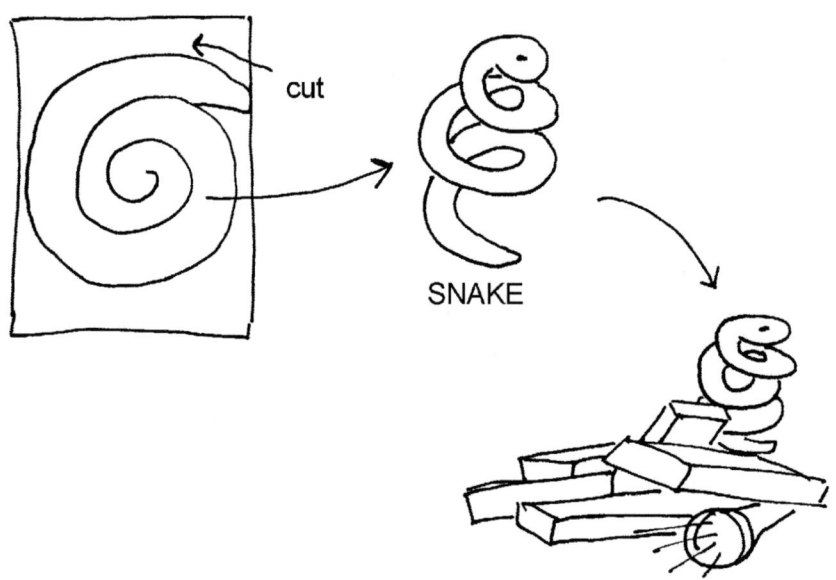

Talk About
1. What is winter like? Is God with us then? What is autumn like? Is God with us then? What is spring like? Is God with us then? What is summer like? Is God with us then?
2. Does God ever leave us?
3. How did God show he was with Paul in our story?

The Church

Fruit of the Spirit
Galatians 5:22-23

Materials
- nine pieces of green construction paper
- scissors
- apple, banana, orange, lemon, lime, grapefruit, pear, peach, plum

Prepare Ahead of Time
- Cut leaves out of each piece of paper. See the pattern on page 180 in the appendix.

While You Tell the Story

Ask nine children to stand up. Ask each one to hold a leaf in one hand, as if they were a tree and their arms were branches. Place a fruit in the other hand. Talk about how you can tell what kind of tree it is by the kind of fruit that it has. Ask the other children to stand up. Pretend you are studying each one carefully. Comment on what you see: love in one child's actions, joy on one child's face, peace, and so on. Say you can tell Jesus is growing them up to be like him, and his Spirit is giving them these different kinds of "fruits" growing in them, the fruit of God's Spirit.

When you are finished with the story, you can make a fruit salad.

Talk About
1. How can you show love? How does joy show in you?
2. What is peace? What is patience? When do you have to be patient?
3. How can you show goodness and kindness and gentleness to others?
4. What is faithfulness? What is self-control?
5. How do you get all of these?

> The Church

Paul Writes Letters
Philippians 4:4-8, 13

Materials
- Bible
- glue or tape
- scissors
- five index cards
- envelope
- markers
- copies of the pictures on page 181 in the appendix

Prepare Ahead of Time
- Copy and cut out the pictures from the pattern in the appendix. Glue one picture on each index card.
- Place the index cards in the envelope. Draw a stamp on it and address it to "The Philippians." For the return address, write "Paul."

While You Tell the Story
   Tell the children how Paul wrote letters to people in different places. We have copies of his letters in our Bibles. Show the book of Philippians in your Bible. "Let's read part of Paul's letter to the Philippians." Ask the children to pretend to be the Philippians. Show them the envelope. Let the children pull index cards out of the envelope one at a time and show everyone. Tell the children what each one means.

   S m i l i n g   f a c e : *Always be full of joy.*

   P r a y i n g   c h i l d : *Don't worry. Instead, pray and give thanks.*

   H e a r t : *God will give us great peace.*

   H e a d : *Think about things that are beautiful and good.*

Talk About
1. What did Paul say we should do?
2. What things should we think about? What is something good to think about?

> The Church

John Sees Heaven
Revelation 21:1-4, 22-27

Materials
- flashlight
- Bible and bookmark
- butcher paper
- crayons, markers

Prepare Ahead of Time
- Place a bookmark in Revelation 21.

While You Tell the Story
    Tell the children to lie down and close their eyes. Turn on the flashlight and turn off the classroom lights. Tell the children that while you read, you want them to imagine and picture what Heaven must be like. Read Revelation 21:1-4, 22-27 from a simple Bible version. Then roll paper out on the floor and let them draw what they saw in their minds as you read.

> **Talk About**
> 1. Who is in Heaven? What is Heaven like? Why does it not need the sun or moon there?
> 2. What do you think you'll tell God when you get to Heaven?
> 3. What do you think you'll say to Jesus?

Storytelling – Appendix A

Story Figures

1. Fashion Dolls (like Barbie)
Make Bible-times clothes from squares of fabric with armholes cut in them. Wrap these around the doll and tie with a strip of fabric or a ribbon.

2. Small Toy Figures
Playmobile-type figures.

3. Paper Dolls
Make Bible-times clothes from paper. Use Velcro strips or clay-like adhesive (Plasti-Tak) to keep the paper clothes on.

4. Dowel Dolls
Make people by cutting 1-inch diameter dowels into varying lengths. Paint features on them or draw features with permanent markers.

5. Wooden Clothespin Figures
Craft stores and discount variety stores sell clothespins that don't have springs. Draw or paint features on them. You may even glue on fabric for clothes.

6. Chenille Wire Figures
Make these figures from chenille wires. Each figure requires two wires. Make a loop in the center of the first wire. Twist it closed. This forms the head and legs. Twist the second wire around the first to make arms.
You may glue or tie on fabric clothes.

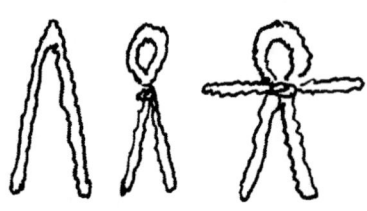

7. Toothpick Figures
Cut out a picture of a character. Tape a toothpick on the back of the picture and stand it up in clay or Styrofoam.

8. Hand Puppets
Sew two pieces of fabric together to make a mitten shape with a thumb and little finger. Draw features. Use yarn for hair.

9. Paper Cup Figures
Turn paper or Styrofoam cups upside down. Small cups can be children or short people. Draw features on the cups. The bottom of a cup can be glued to the bottom of another cup to make a crown.

10. Hanky Dolls
Roll the left and right sides of a handkerchief toward the center. Fold the top down a few inches from the bottom. Tie a ribbon or string an inch or two from the top. Draw features with a permanent marker. To make an angel, spread out the short-rolled sides for arms, and bring the short end back up around the head.

Storytelling - Appendix A

11. Clothespin Animal
Clip two spring-type clothespins to the bottom of an animal body. (See pattern on page 161 of the appendix.)

12. Pretzel Camel
Use a large pretzel. Twist Chenille wires around the bottom side as shown. Stand the camels up in clay.

13. Box Figures
Make these out of boxes shaped like rice boxes or cereal boxes. Draw a V shape on the back of the box. Draw a large circle close to the bottom of the front. Cut down the sides of the box at each corner so the box lies flat. Cut out around the circle, leaving the circle attached. Cut out the V shape. Staple an index card on the back as shown. Slip your hand under the index card to hold up the figure. If the box is a small cereal box, cut the index card to fit the figure and slip a finger under it to hold the figure.

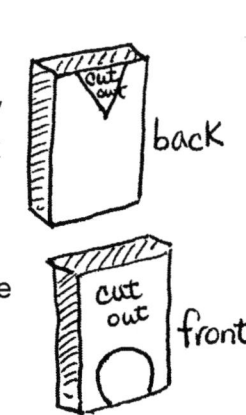

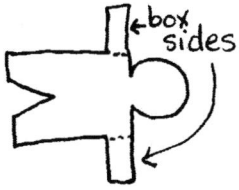
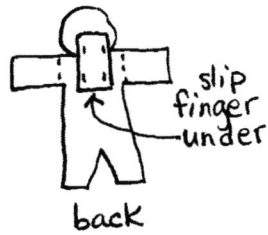

14. Spoon Figures
Draw a face on the bowl of a plastic spoon. Twist a chenille wire around the handle close to the bowl to make arms.

15. Envelope Donkeys
Cut an envelope as shown in the pattern. Bend the two sides of the neck up. Spread the legs slightly so it will stand. Tape the sides of the head together.

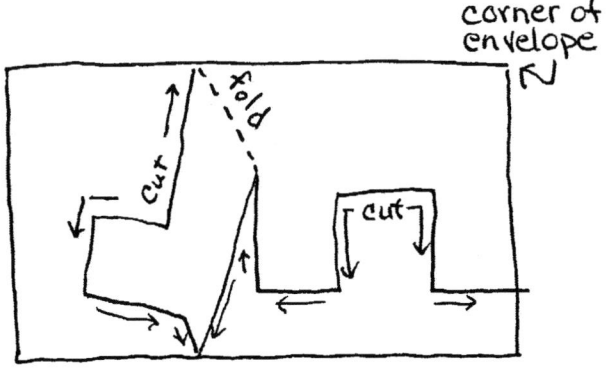

Storytelling – Appendix B

Shadow Theater

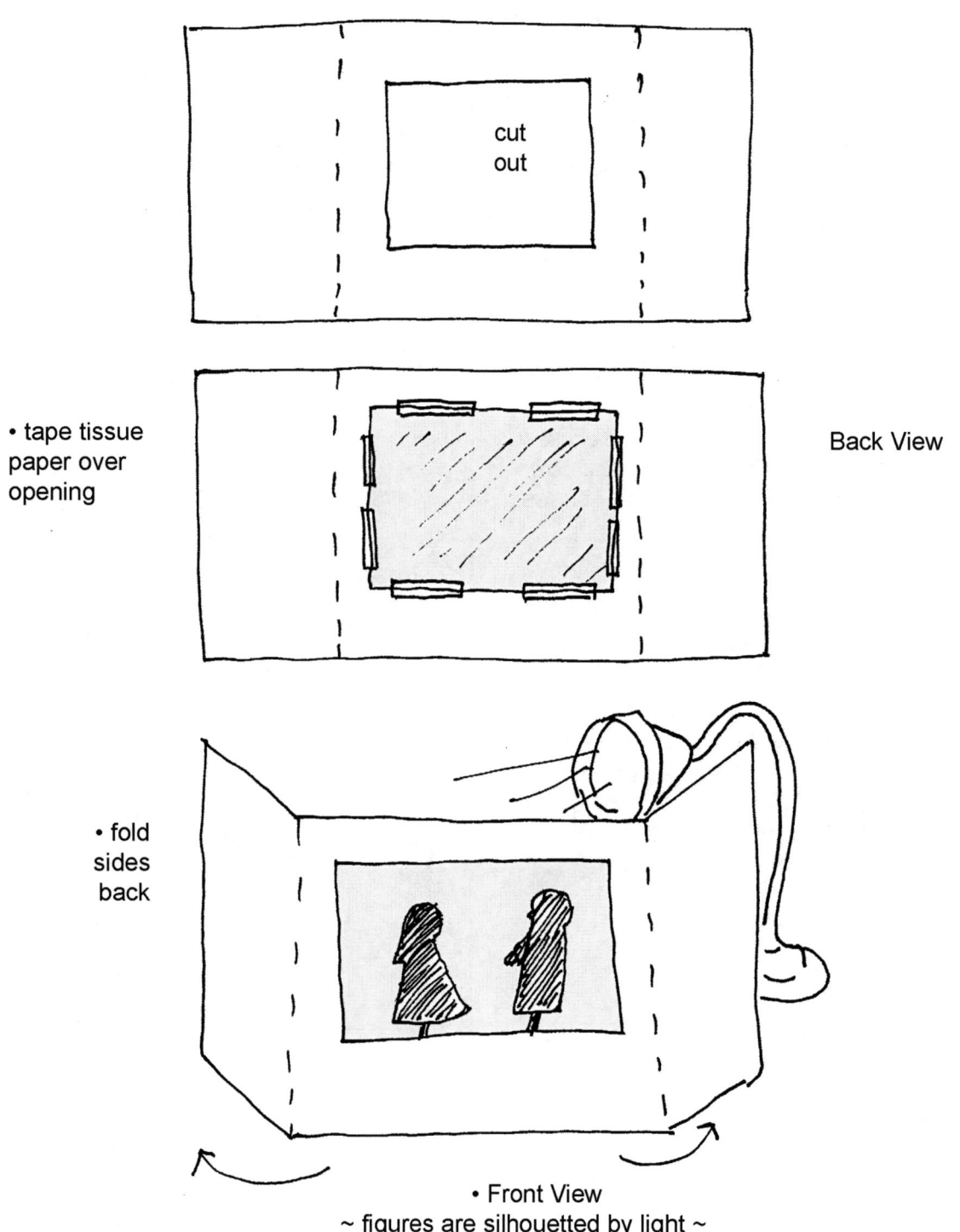

Storytelling - Appendix C

Appendices

You have permission to photocopy the illustrations
in this appendix for classroom use.

- Leaving the Garden — 158
- Joseph's Dreams — 159
- Burning Bush — 160
- The Plagues in Egypt — 161
- Deborah — 162
- Samson and Delilah — 163
- David and Goliath — 164
- Ravens Feed Elijah — 165
- Elisha's Servant Sees God's Army — 166
- Daniel and the Lions — 167
- Jesus Is Born — 168
- Jesus Makes Breakfast for His Friends — 169
- Jesus Goes Back to Heaven — 170
- The Great Catch of Fish — 171
- Tax Money in a Fish — 172
- Blind Bartimaeus — 173
- Birds and Flowers — 174
- The Lord's Prayer — 175
- Zacchaeus — 176
- Peter and John Heal a Lame Man — 177
- Philip and the Man From Ethiopia — 178
- Peter Escapes From Prison — 179
- Fruit of the Spirit — 180
- Paul Writes Letters — 181

Storytelling – Appendix C
Leaving the Garden

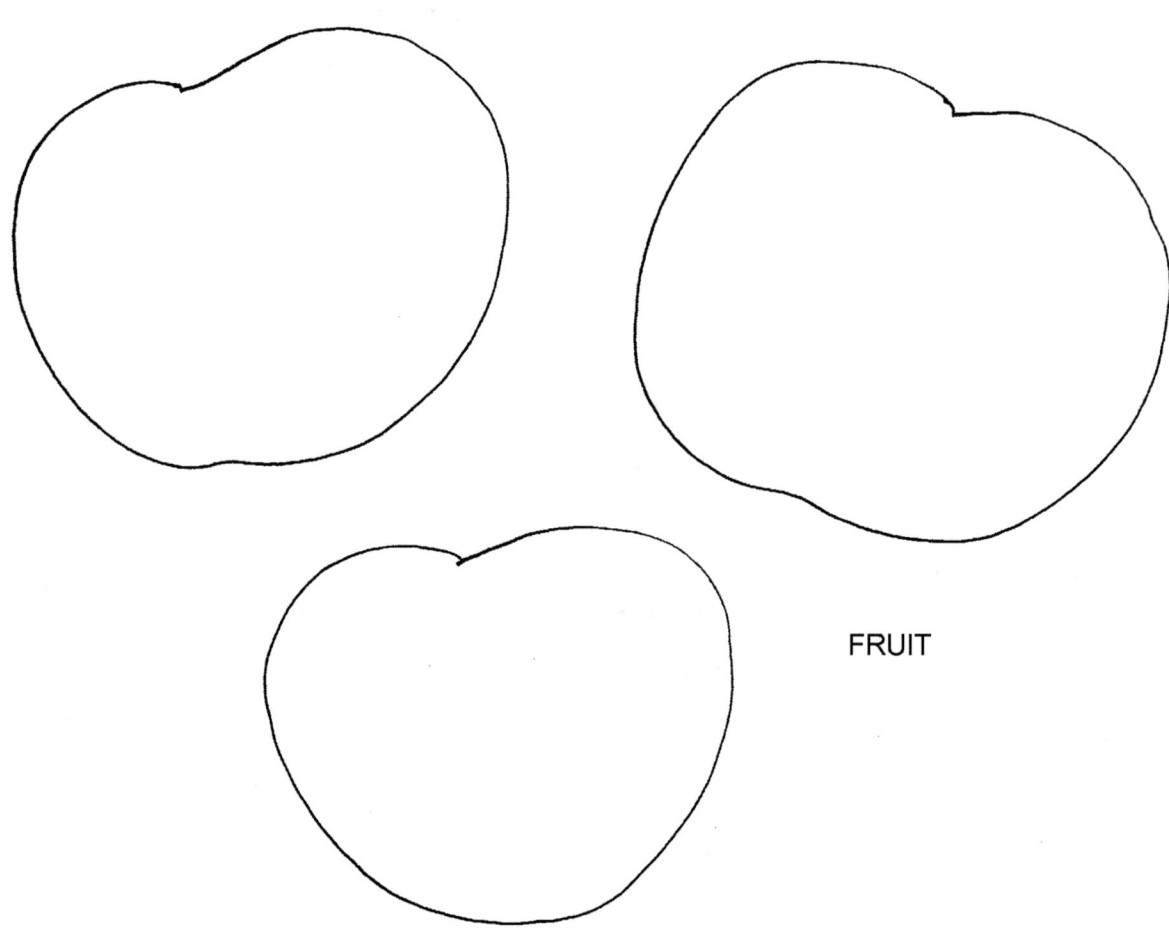

FRUIT

Make posterboard trees:

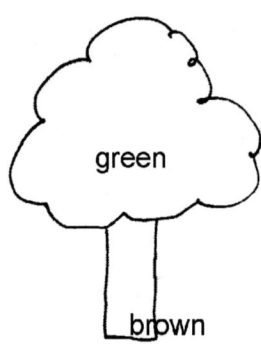

Makd a spiral snake:

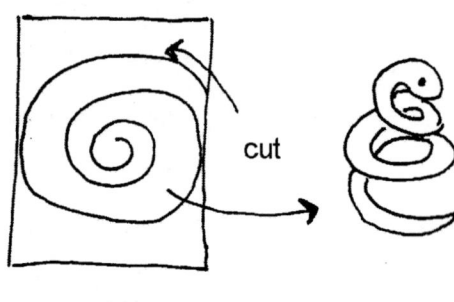

construction paper

Storytelling – Appendix C

Joseph's Dreams

Storytelling – Appendix C

Burning Bush

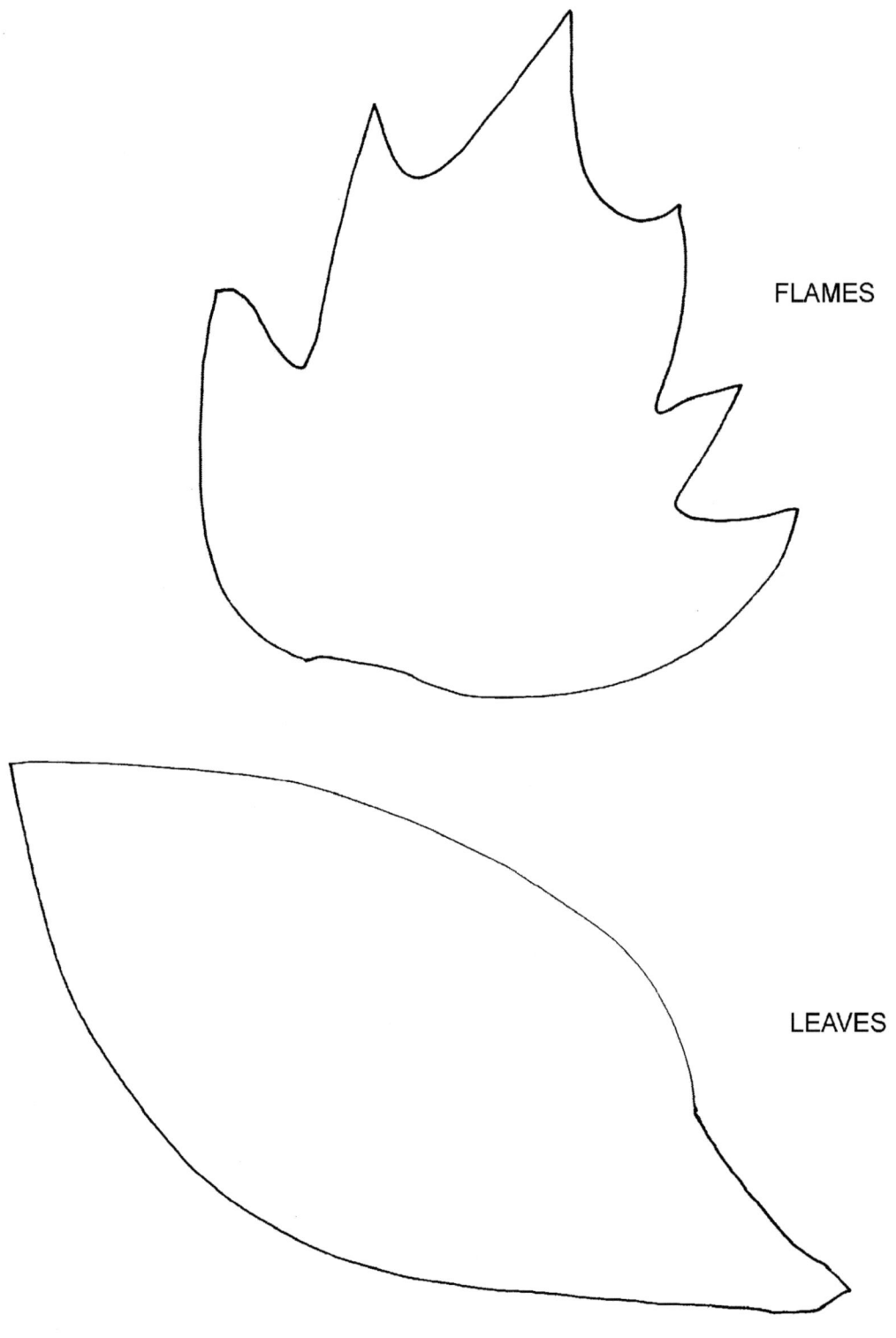

FLAMES

LEAVES

Storytelling - Appendix C

The Plagues in Egypt

Follow these instructions as you tell the story:

1. Blood: Show the jar of red water. Tell the children it's not real blood.	6. Boils: Sprinkle baby powder on the children's arms to represent "skin sickness."
2. Frogs: Hop the toy frog around the group or scatter the green paper circles around the room.	7. Hail: Show the jar of rock salt.
3. Gnats: Pour the black paper circles into your hand. Toss them into the air.	8. Locusts: Fly the toy insect around the children or toss out the black "winged" triangles.
4. Flies: Fly the toy fly around the children, or use the brown paper triangles as you used the black circles.	9. Darkness: Turn off the lights or ask the children to cover their eyes.
5. Cows: Set the cow figure(s) up, but then make them fall over.	10. Firstborn deaths: Tell about this. Tell how God kept his people safe through all of these back troubles. Finally, Pharaoh let God's people go.

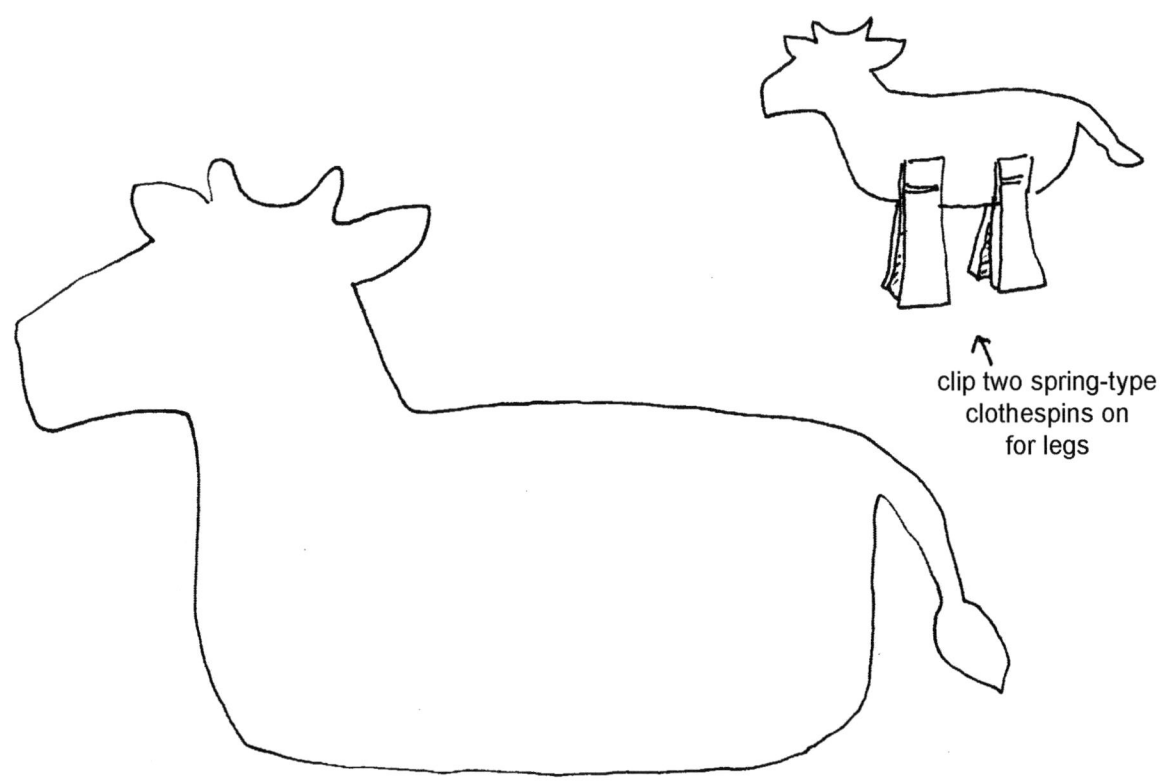

clip two spring-type clothespins on for legs

161

Storytelling – Appendix C

Deborah

NOTE: to make the leaf larger or smaller, use the enlarge or reduce feature on a photocopy machine.

Storytelling - Appendix C

Samson and Delilah

1.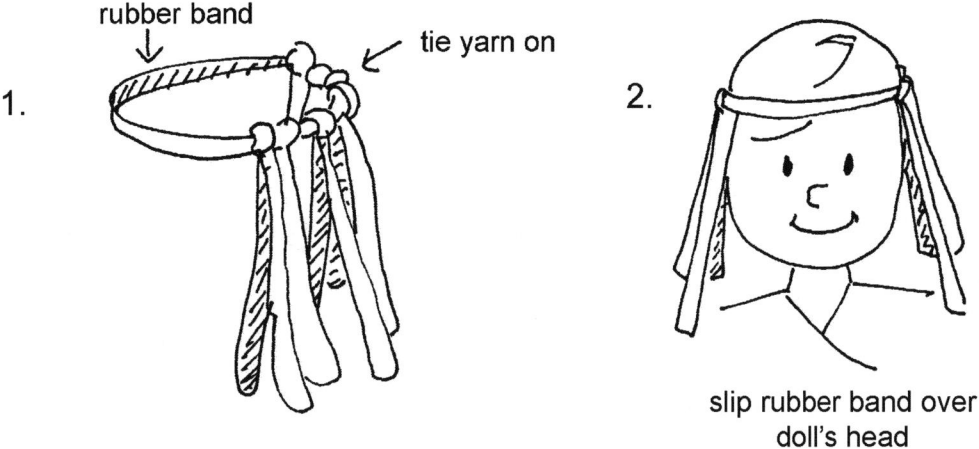

2. slip rubber band over doll's head

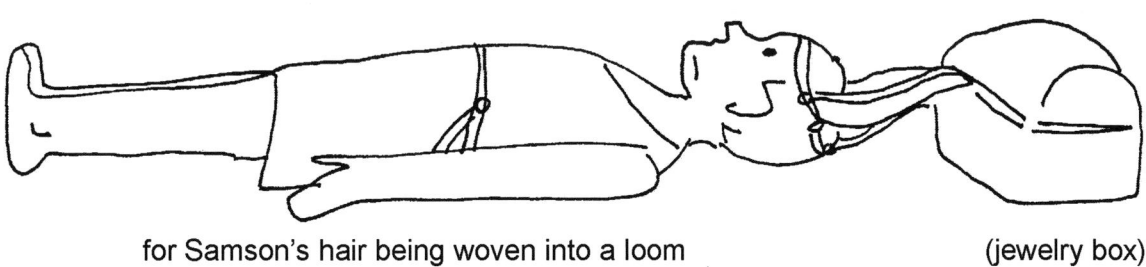

for Samson's hair being woven into a loom   (jewelry box)

163

Storytelling - Appendix C

David and Goliath

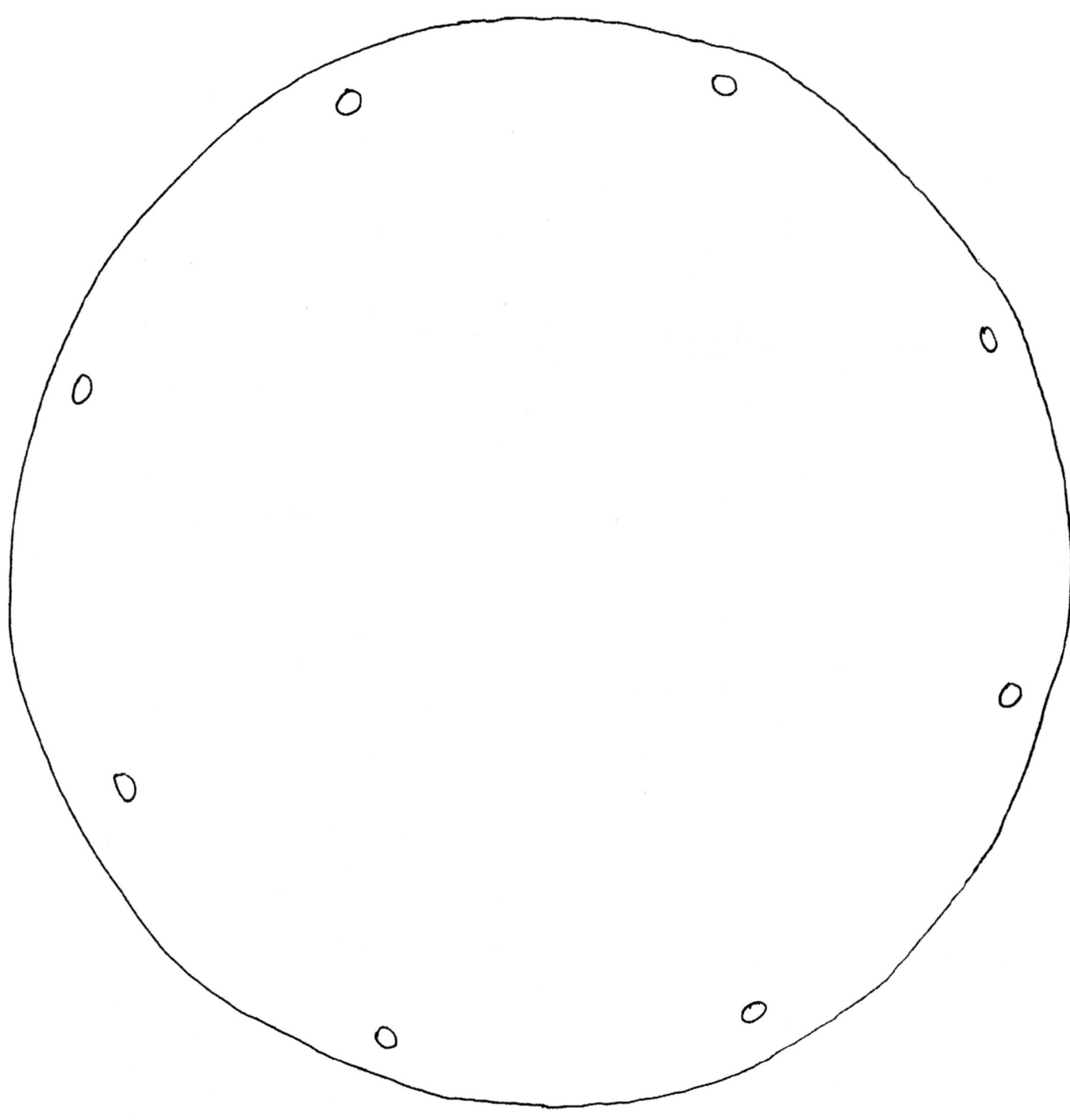

164

Storytelling - Appendix C

Ravens Feed Elijah

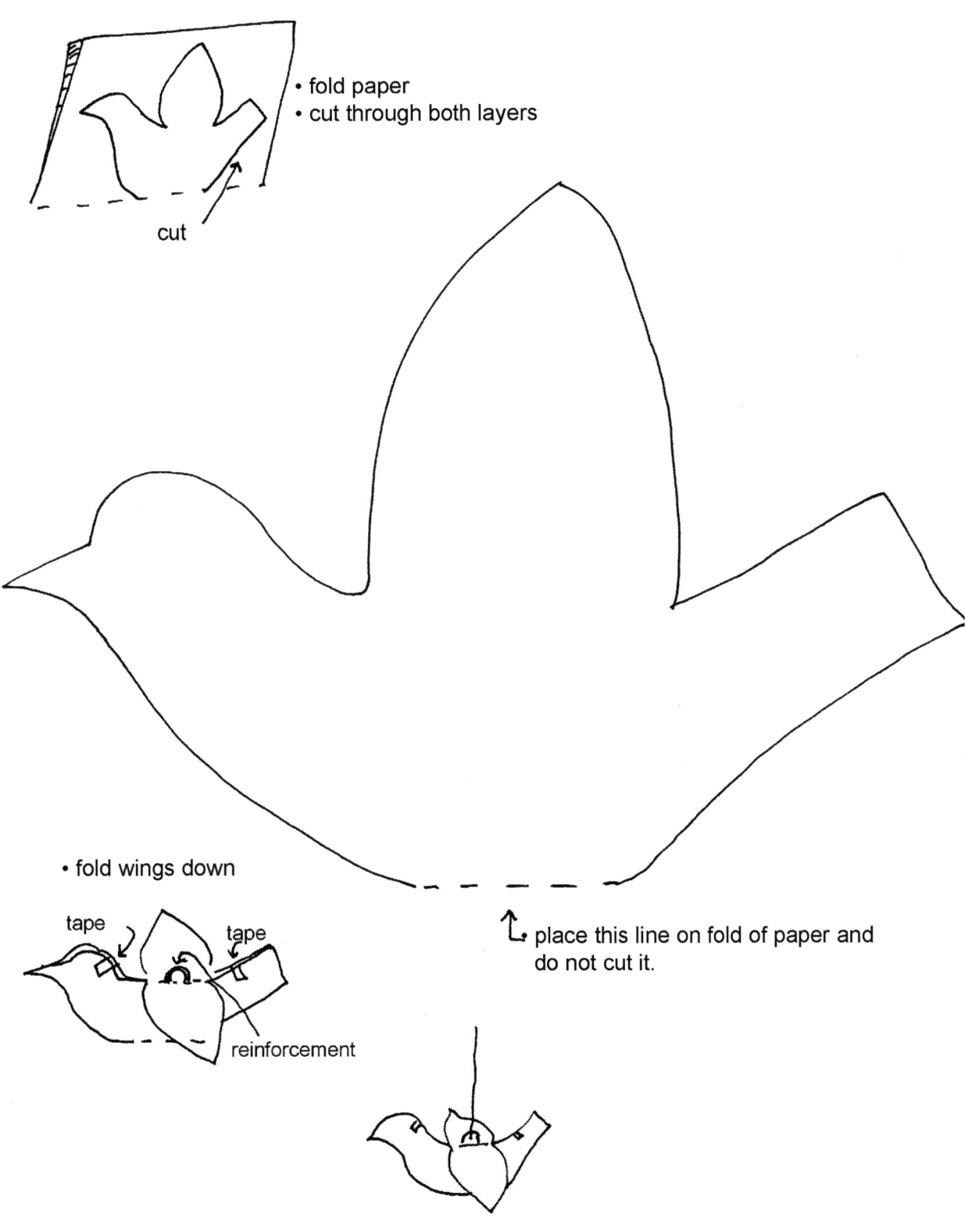

- fold paper
- cut through both layers

cut

- fold wings down

tape   tape

reinforcement

⤴ place this line on fold of paper and do not cut it.

165

Storytelling – Appendix C

Elisha's Servant Sees God's Army

166

Storytelling – Appendix C
Daniel and the Lions

Storytelling – Appendix C

Jesus Is Born

When unfolded, the figure will be a manger scene in silhouette:

Suggestion: If you cut the scene from dark paper, tape it to a full sheet of light paper. If you cut it from light paper, tape it to dark paper.

• cut on solid line

• place dotted edge at fold of paper

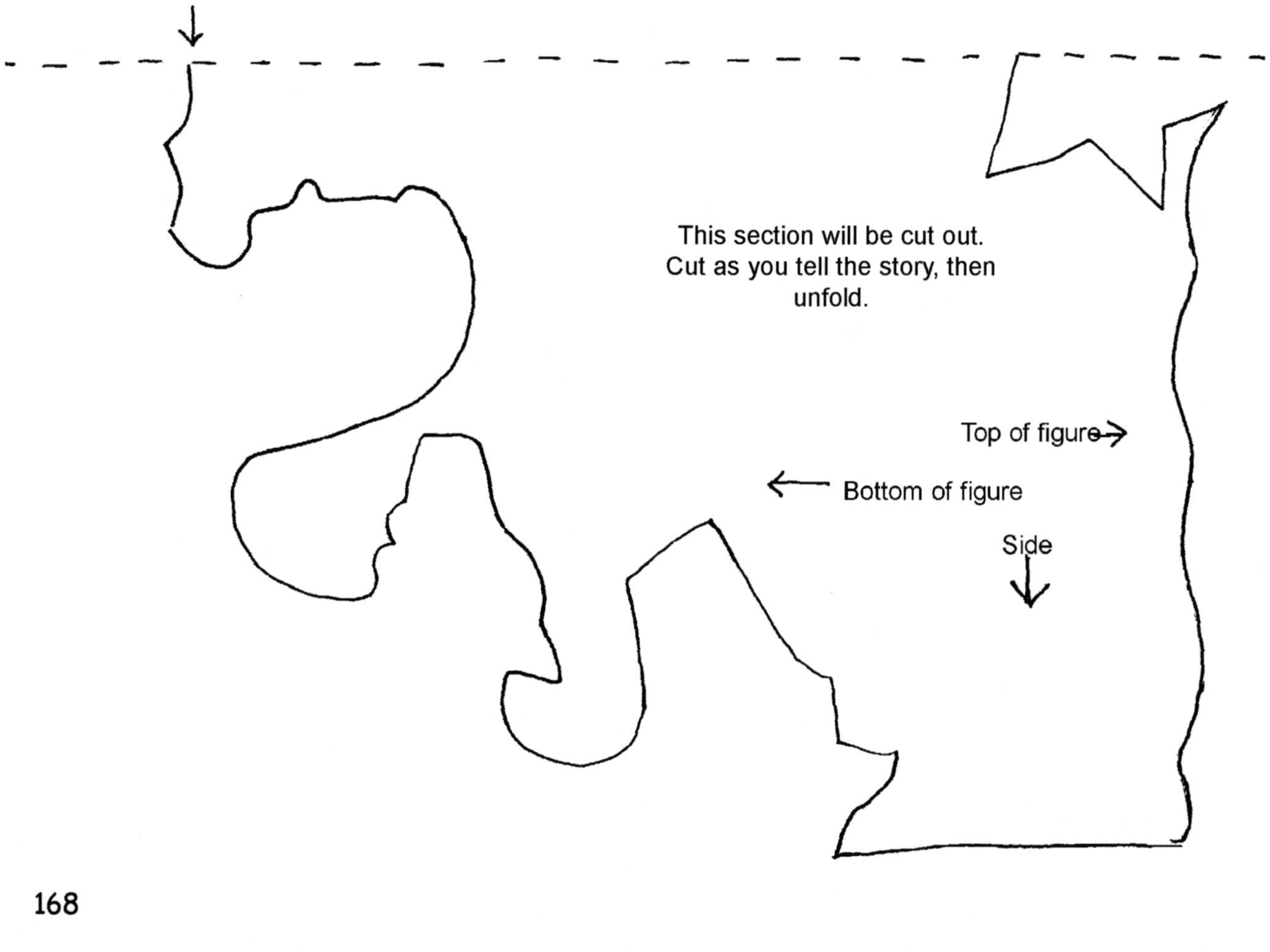

This section will be cut out. Cut as you tell the story, then unfold.

Top of figure →

← Bottom of figure

Side ↓

168

Storytelling – Appendix C

Jesus Makes Breakfast for His Friends

Storytelling - Appendix C

Jesus Goes Back to Heaven

Storytelling – Appendix C

The Great Catch of Fish

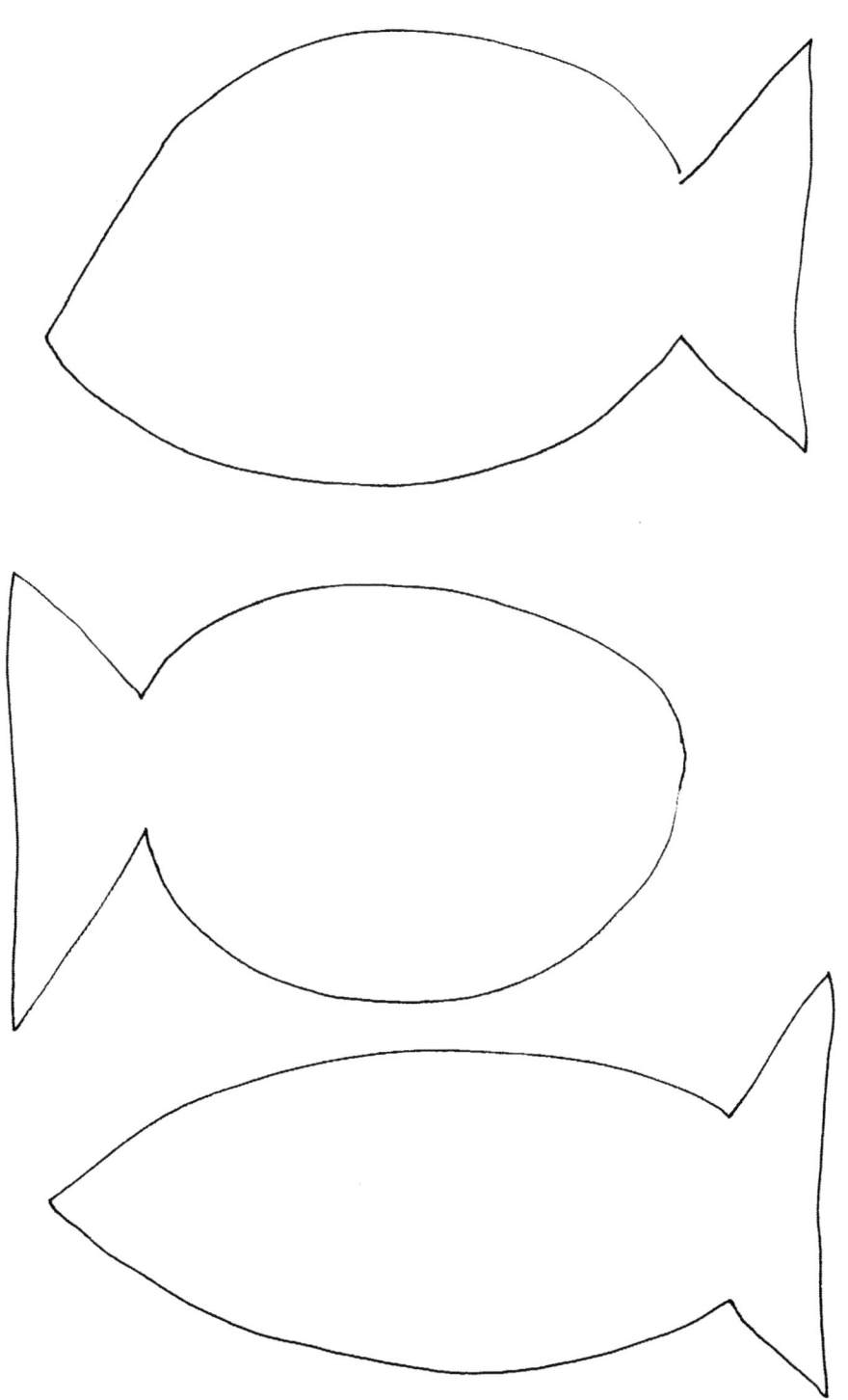

Storytelling – Appendix C

Tax Money in a Fish

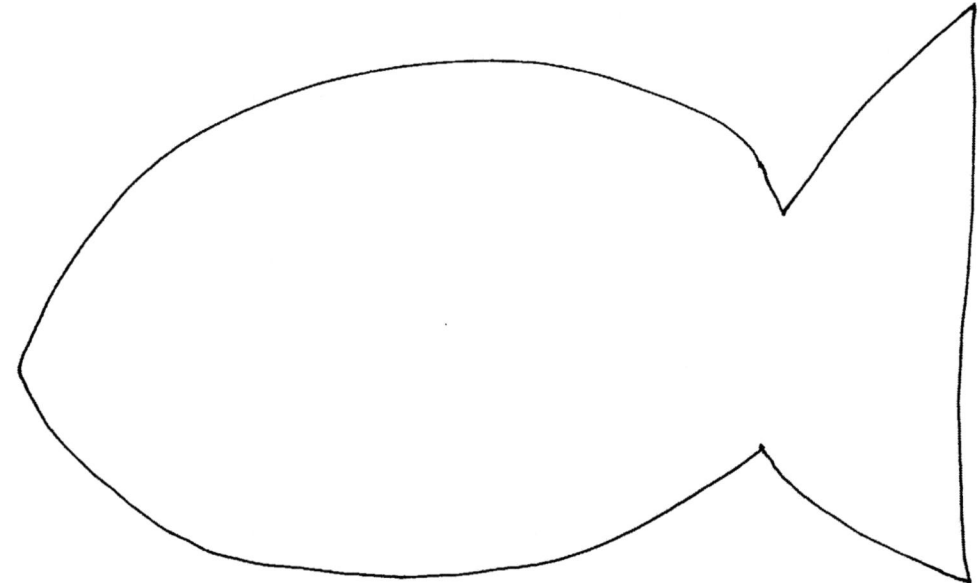

Storytelling – Appendix C

Blind Bartimaeus

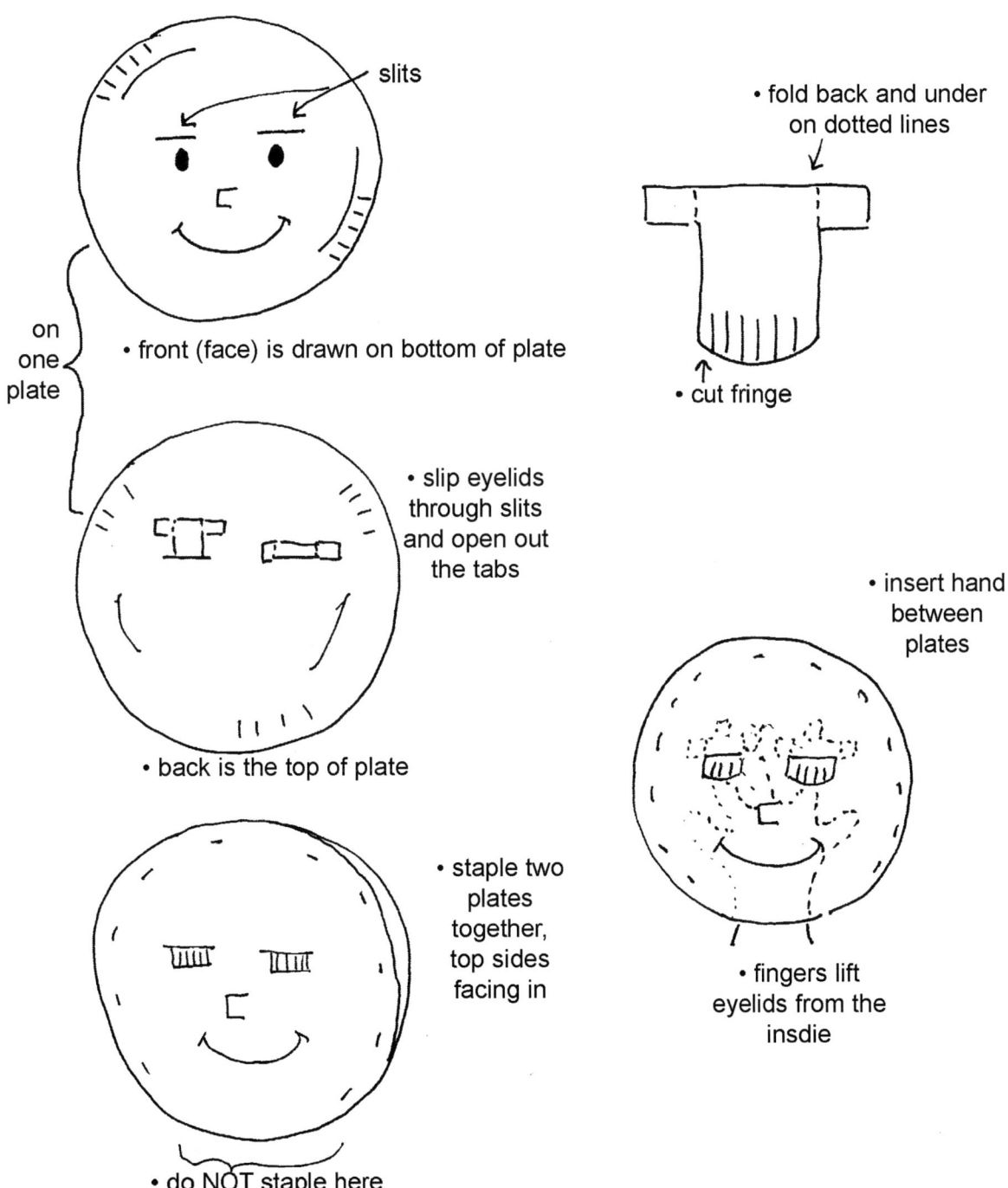

- front (face) is drawn on bottom of plate
- on one plate
- slits
- slip eyelids through slits and open out the tabs
- back is the top of plate
- staple two plates together, top sides facing in
- do NOT staple here
- fold back and under on dotted lines
- cut fringe
- insert hand between plates
- fingers lift eyelids from the insdie

173

Storytelling – Appendix C

Birds and Flowers

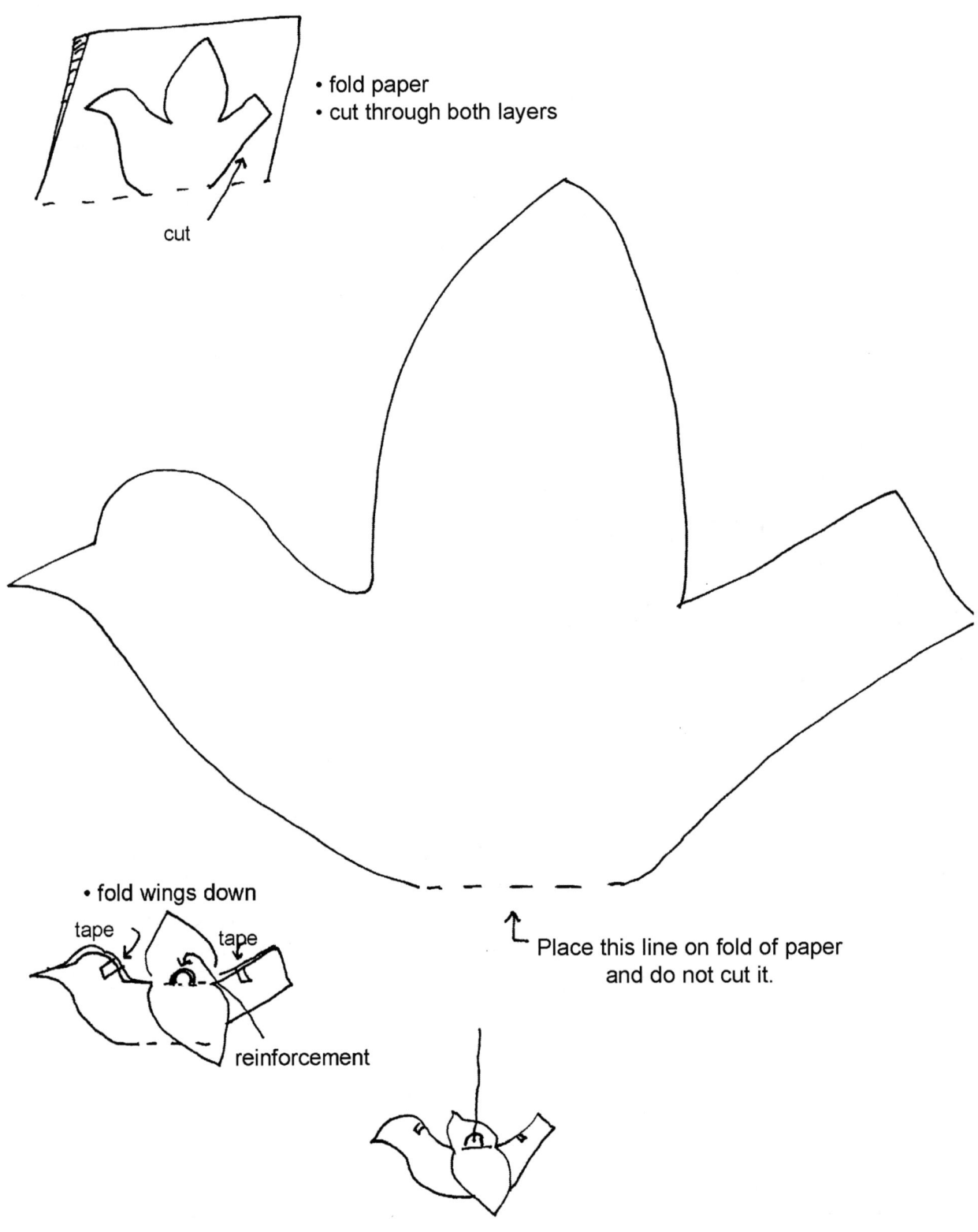

- fold paper
- cut through both layers

cut

- fold wings down

tape tape

reinforcement

Place this line on fold of paper and do not cut it.

Storytelling – Appendix C

The Lord's Prayer

Storytelling - Appendix C

Zacchaeus

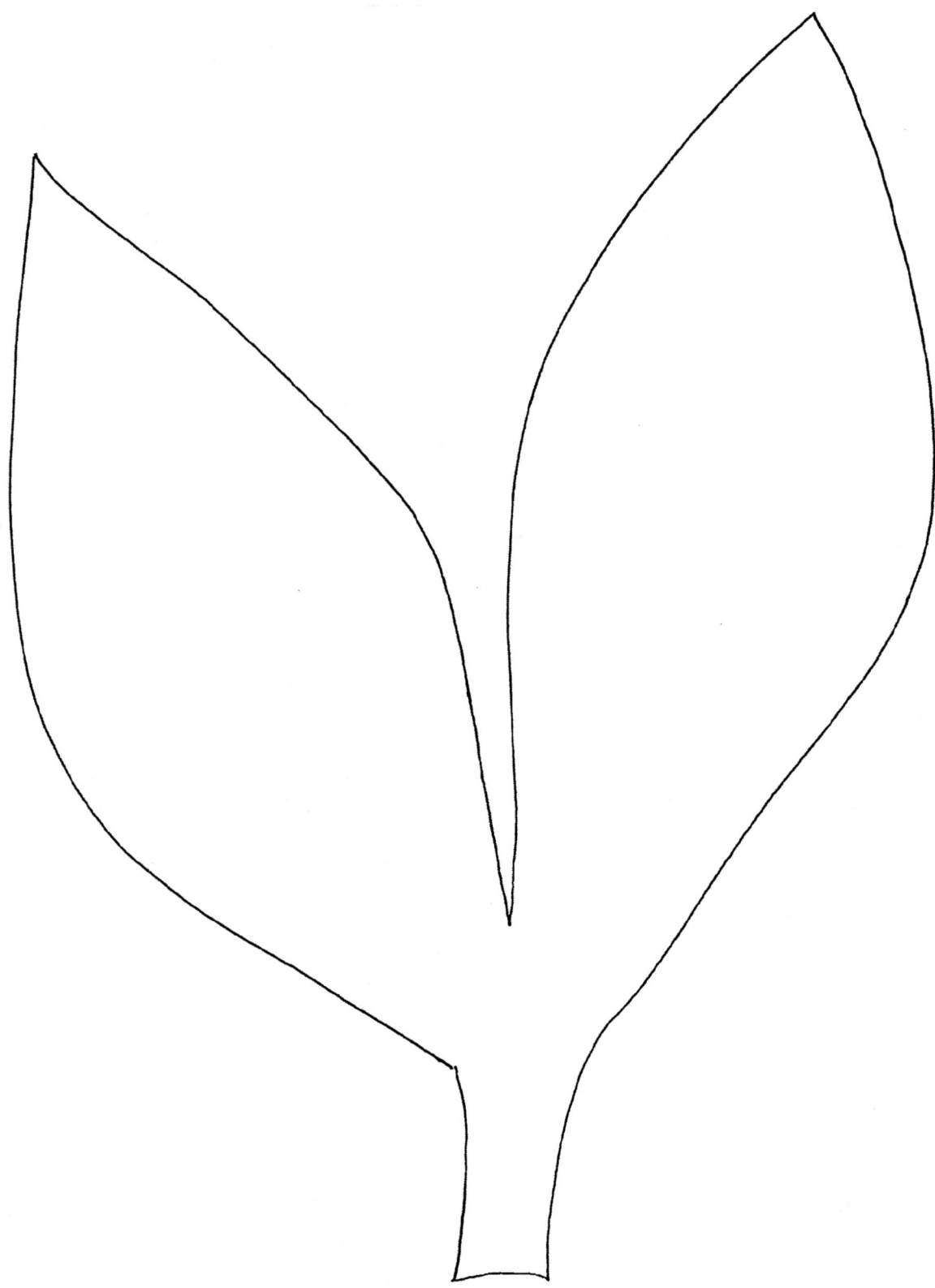

Storytelling – Appendix C

Peter and John Heal a Lame Man

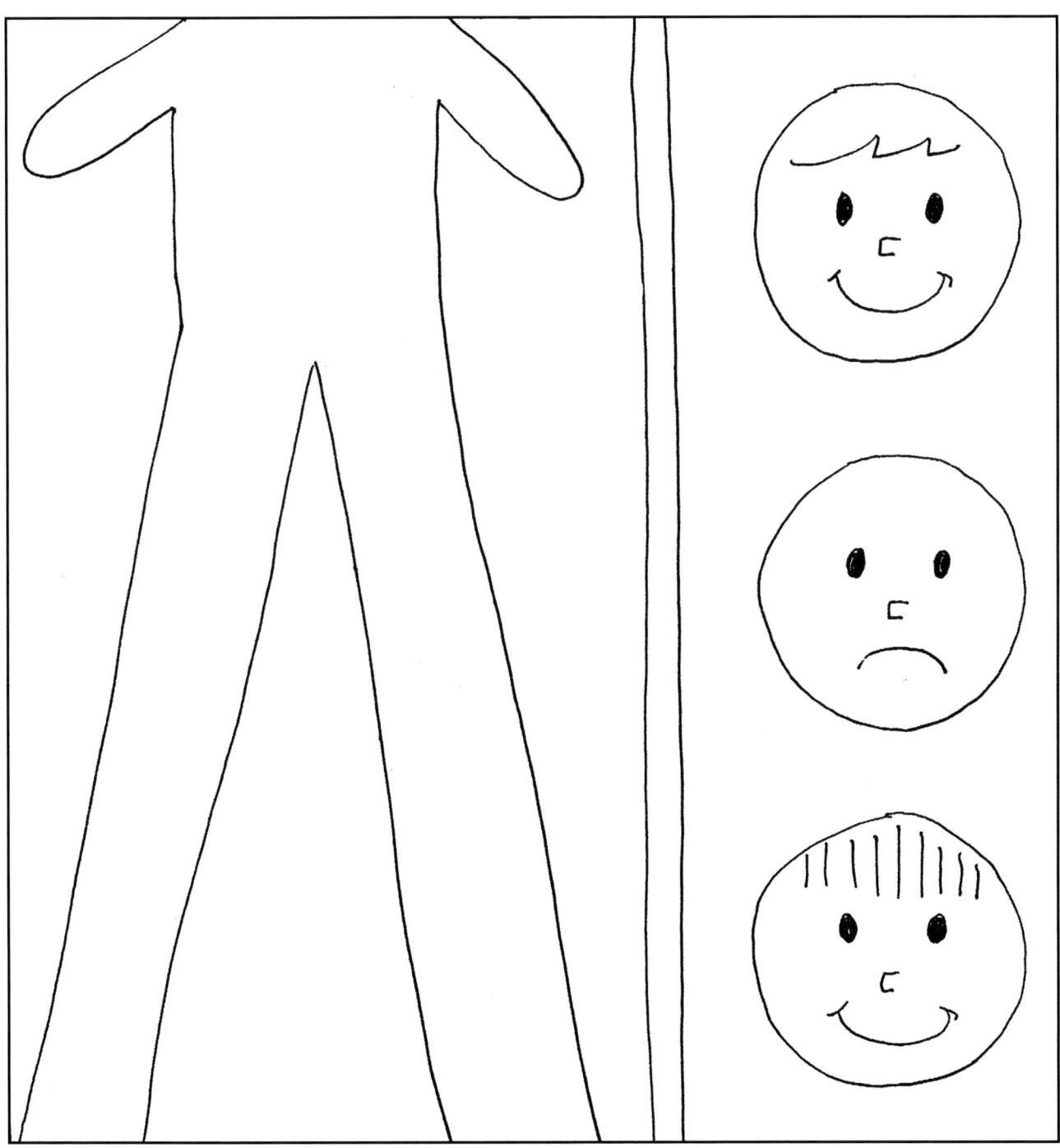

177

Storytelling - Appendix C

Philip and the Man From Ethiopia

1.

2.

3.

4.

5.

6.

• draw on front

• turn it over and draw sections

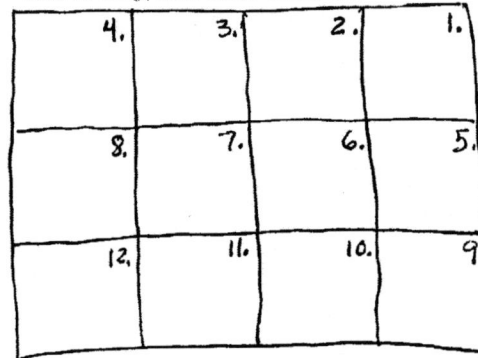

• draw one picture in each section, matching them by number, OR photocopy these pictures and glue them in their sections.

• cut the sections apart.

• as you read or tell the story, ask children to lay the sections down in this order:

... so when they are turned over, the front picture appears.

7.

8.

9.

10. Jesus

11.

12.

178

Storytelling – Appendix C

Peter Escapes From Prison

1. Peter was sleeping, chained between two guards.

2. Suddenly an angel came and a bright light shone down.

3. "Quick! Get up," said the angel. The chains fell off.

4. The angel said, "Put on your clothes and sandals." And Peter did.

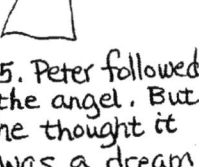
5. Peter followed the angel. But he thought it was a dream.

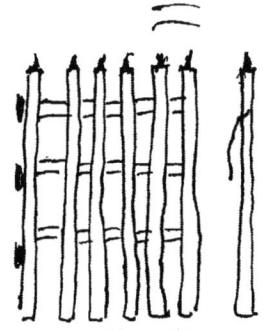
6. When they came to the prison gate, it opened by itself. They walked through, and the angel left.

7. Peter went to Mary's house where his friends were praying. He knocked on the door.

8. Rhoda ran to answer. When she heard Peter's voice, she was so excited, she ran to tell everyone and forgot to open the door!

9. Peter kept knocking until they let him in.

10. Peter's friends were surprised to see him. He told them everything that had happened.

Storytelling – Appendix C

Fruit of the Spirit

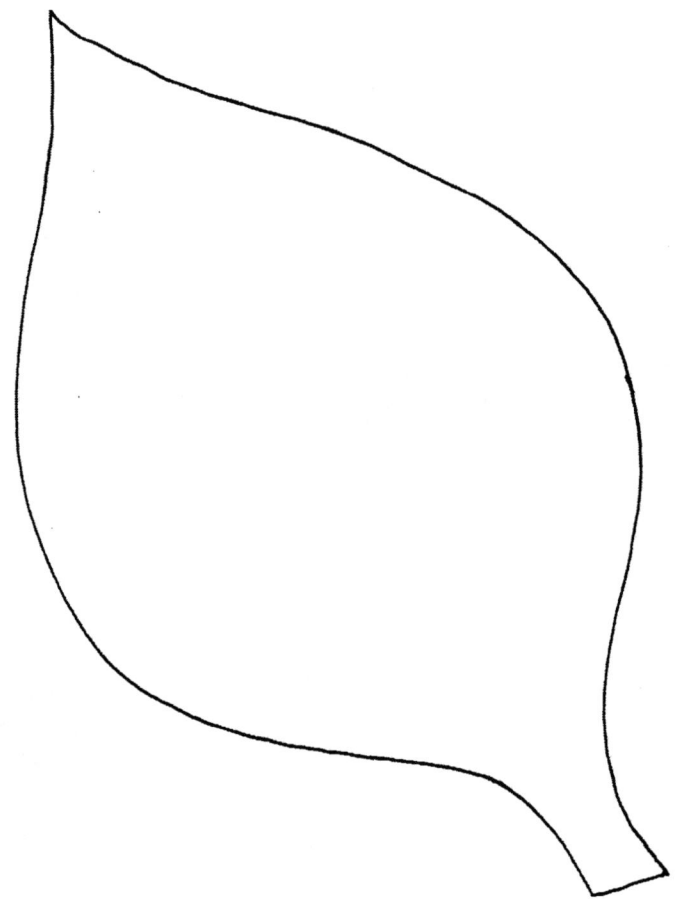

Storytelling – Appendix C

Paul Writes Letters

Topical Index

Angels
    Angels Appear to the Shepherds   86
    Balaam's Donkey   36
    Gabriel Appears to Mary   83
    Peter Escapes From Prison   143
    Philip and the Man From Ethiopia   137

Animals
    Adam Names the Animals   6
    Angels Appear to the Shepherds   86
    Balaam's Donkey   36
    Creation of Animals and People   4
    David, the Shepherd   51
    Jesus Is Born   85
    Rachel's Sheep   19
    Solomon Knows About Animals   57
    The Lost Sheep   127

Birds
    Adam Names the Animals   6
    Birds and Flowers   119
    Creation of Animals and People   4
    Ravens Feed Elijah   59

Boats
    Jesus Stills the Storm   107
    Jonah   81
    Noah and the Ark   9
    Paul's Shipwreck   149

Christmas
    Angels Appear to the Shepherds   86
    Gabriel Appears to Mary   83
    Jesus Is Born   85
    Mary Praises God   84
    The Wise Men   87

Colors
    Creation of Plants   3
    Joseph's Colorful Coat   20

Creation
    Creation of Animals and People   4
    Creation of Earth, Sky, and Sea   2
    Creation of Plants   3
    The Garden of Eden   5

Easter
    Jesus' Death and Resurrection   96
    Jesus Goes Back to Heaven   99
    Jesus Meets Friends on the Road to Emmaus   97
    The Lord's Supper   95
    The Triumphal Entry   93

Families
    A Widow's Oil Jars   65
    Abraham and Lot   11
    Adam and Eve, Cain and Abel   7
    Baby Moses   25
    Jacob and Esau   15
    Jesus Grew   89
    Joseph's Dreams   21
    Joseph's Silver Cup   24
    Paul's Nephew Hears a Plot   148
    Recab's Family   75
    Ruth   44
    The Promise of Isaac   13
    The Runaway Son   129
    Timothy   145

Fish
    Creation of Animals and People   4
    Jesus Feeds 5,000   110
    Tax Money in a Fish   112
    The Great Catch of Fish   101

Food
    Abigail Packs Food   54
    Abraham and the Three Visitors   12
    A Widow Shares With Elijah   60
    Daniel Refuses the King's Food   76
    Elisha and the Stew   67
    Jesus Feeds 5,000   110
    Jesus Makes Breakfast for His Friends   98
    John the Baptist   90
    Manna and Quail   31
    Ravens Feed Elijah   59
    The Lord's Supper   95
    Water Into Wine   100

Forgiveness

Topical Index

Joseph's Silver Cup	24

Friends

David and Jonathan	53
Deborah	39
Elijah Goes Up to Heaven	64
Jesus Chooses Twelve Friends	92
Paul and Barnabas	140
Paul in a Basket	139
Peter and Cornelius	142
Queen of Sheba	58
Samson and Delilah	43
Through the Roof	103

Giving and Gifts

Joseph's Colorful Coat	20
Solomon's Dream	56
The Widow's Mite	135

God's Power and God's Word

David and Goliath	52
Elijah on Mount Carmel	61
Elisha's Servant Sees God's Army	69
Ezra Reads God's Words	74
Jesus Reads in the Synagogue	117
King Josiah Finds God's Word	71
Sower of Seeds	123
The Plagues in Egypt	27
The Sun Stands Still	38
The Ten Commandments	32
Twelve Spies	34
Zechariah Cannot Speak	82

God's Protection

Birds and Flowers	119
Crossing the Red Sea	28
Daniel and the Lions	80
David, the Shepherd	51
Deborah	39
Elijah and the Cloud	62
Elijah in a Cave	63
Elisha's Servant Sees God's Army	69
Gideon and the Torches	42
Gideon's Men	41
God Talks to Isaac	16
Jacob's Dream	18
Jehoshaphat's Army	72
Jericho's Walls Fall Down	37
Jesus Stills the Storm	107
Jesus Walks on Water	111
Jonah	81
Noah and the Ark	9
Paul on Malta	150
Samuel Hears God	47
Shadrach, Meshach, and Abednego	78

God's Provision

Bitter Water Turns Sweet	30
Burning Bush	26
David and Goliath	52
Isaac Gets a Wife	14
Jesus Feeds 5,000	110
Manna and Quail	31
More Dreams	23
Ravens Feed Elijah	59
Tax Money in a Fish	112
The Promise of Isaac	13

Growing/My Body

Daniel Refuses the King's Food	76
Jesus as a Boy in the Temple	88
Jesus Grew	89
Jesus Washes His Friends' Feet	94
Jonathan Eats Honey	48
Samuel's New Coats	46

Heaven

Elijah Goes Up to Heaven	64
Jesus Goes Back to Heaven	99
John Sees Heaven	153

Healing/Sickness

Blind Bartimaeus	115
Jairus' Daughter	109
Jesus Heals the Bent Woman	114
King Hezekiah Gets Well	70
Naaman	68
Peter's Mother-in-Law	102
The Centurion's Sick Servant	106
The Lame Man at the Pool	104
The Man's Withered Hand	105
The Ten Lepers	113
Through the Roof	103
Woman Touches Jesus' Hem	108

Topical Index

Helping/Serving
A Widow's Oil Jars	65
Adam and Eve, Cain and Abel	7
Baby Moses	25
Building the Tabernacle	33
Dorcas	141
Jesus heals the Bent Woman	114
Jesus Washes His Friend's Feet	94
Joseph at Potiphar's House	22
Paul in Lystra	144
Philip and the Man From Ethiopia	138
Ruth	44
Samuel's New Coats	46
Timothy	145

Home/Where I Live
Abraham and Lot	11
Elisha's Room on the Roof	66
Samuel's New Coats	46
Taking Care of the Worship House	73

Jesus Is Our Friend
Jesus and the Children	131
Jesus Makes Breakfast for His Friends	98
Mary and Martha	126
Zacchaeus	132

Kindness
David and Mephibosheth	55
Elisha's Room on the Roof	66
Fruit of the Spirit	151
Joseph's Dreams	21
Lydia	146
Paul and Silas in Prison	147
The Great Catch of Fish	101

Land, Sea, and Sky
Abraham and Lot	11
Creation of Earth, Sky, and Sea	2
The Great Catch of Fish	101
The Sun Stands Still	38

Leaders
Aaron's Staff Blooms	35
Daniel and the Lions	80
David Is Anointed	49
Deborah	39
The Plagues in Egypt	27

Listening
Burning Bush	26
Elijah in a Cave	63
Mary and Martha	126
Paul's Nephew Hears a Plot	148
Samuel Hears God	47
The Wise Man's House	121
Zechariah Cannot Speak	82

Love
David and Jonathan	53
David Is Anointed	49
Fruit of the Spirit	151
Hidden Treasure	124
Jesus' Death and Resurrection	96

Night (Stars, Moon)
Gideon and the Torches	42
God Talks to Isaac	16
Samuel Hears God	47
The Wise Men	87

Obeying
Balaam's Donkey	36
Daniel and the Lions	80
Elisha's Room on the Roof	66
Fruit of the Spirit	151
Jericho's Walls Fall Down	37
Jesus As a Boy in the Temple	88
Jesus Is Tempted	91
Jonah	81
King Josiah Finds God's Word	71
Leaving the Garden	8
More Dreams	23
Naaman	68
Paul to Damascus	138
Recab's Family	75
Shadrach, Meshach, and Abednego	78
The Lost Coin	128
The Lost Sheep	127
The Runaway Son	129
The Ten Commandments	32

Topical Index

    The Wise Man's House   121
    Two Sons and a Vineyard   134

People
    Creation of Animals and People   4

Plants and Flowers
    Aaron's Staff Blooms   35
    Birds and Flowers   119
    Creation of Plants   3
    Elisha and the Stew   67

Praise/Worship
    David Plays His Harp   50
    Israelites Praise God After Crossing the Red Sea   29
    Jehoshaphat's Army   72
    Mary Praises God   84
    Paul and Silas in Prison   147
    Perfume on Jesus' Feet   133
    Peter and John Heal a Lame Man   136
    Queen of Sheba   58
    The Lord's Supper   95
    The Runaway Son   129
    The Wise Men   87
    The Woman at the Well   116
    Writing on the Wall   79

Prayer
    Elijah and the Cloud   62
    Elijah on Mount Carmel   61
    Gideon's Fleece   40
    Hannah and Samuel   45
    Isaac Gets a Wife   14
    Jairus' Daughter   109
    More Dreams   23
    Peter Escapes From Prison   143
    Solomon's Dream   56
    The Lord's Prayer   120
    The Pharisee and Tax Collector Pray   130
    The Promise of Isaac   13
    Zacchaeus   132

Sharing
    A Widow Shares With Elijah   60
    Abigail Packs Food   54

    Abraham and Lot   11
    Abraham and the Three Visitors   12
    Bigger Barns   122
    David and Jonathan   53

Soldiers/Armies
    Elisha's Servant Sees God's Army   69
    Gideon's Men   41
    Jehoshaphat's Army   72
    Jericho's Walls Fall Down   37

Thankfulness
    Aaron's Staff Blooms   35
    Daniel Thanks God   77
    Hezekiah Gets Well   70
    Paul's Shipwreck   149
    Paul Writes Letters   152
    The Ten Lepers   113

Traveling
    Jesus Meets Friends on the Road to Emmaus   97
    Paul to Damascus   139
    The Wise Men   87

Truthfulness
    Jacob Deceives Isaac   17
    Leaving the Garden   8

Water
    Bitter Water Turns Sweet   30
    Crossing the Red Sea   28
    Noah and the Ark   9
    Water Into Wine   100

Weather
    Elijah and the Cloud   62
    Jesus Stills the Storm   107
    Jesus Walks on Water   111
    Noah and the Ark   9

Working/Cooperation
    Building the Tabernacle   33
    Joseph at Potiphar's House   22
    Taking Care of the Worship House   73
    Tower of Babel   10

MUSIC AND MOVEMENT FOR PRESCHOOL:
Karyn Henley's PLAYSONGS® DVDs

In this delightful series, Karyn guides young children (2-5 years) as they explore the world around them. Ideal for home, school or day-care. Age-appropriate, interactive and -- most importantly -- FUN!

Each DVD contains 2 half-hour programs for 1 full hour of music and storytelling fun!

FIVE LITTLE LADYBUGS: Children feel the joy of being alive in God's wonderful world.

GROW, GROW, GROW: Celebrates the excitement of gaining new skills and knowledge.

PLDVD1 . . . $14.95

I FEEL LIKE A GIGGLE: Celebrates the joy of being God's child.

DOWN BY THE STATION: Children learn the purpose of obedience and joy of following God's plan.

PLDVD2 . . . $14.95

NOAH'S ZOO: Children are introduced to the delight of praising and worshiping God.

TINY TREASURES: Children discover the joy of being God's most valuable creation.

PLCDVD3 . . . $14.95

Audio and Video samples available on-line, or to order:

KarynHenley.com   1-888-573-3953